Science and heart:
The triumph of psychosocial care
in pediatrics

Also by Thomas McCormally
For All Children Everywhere: Children's Mercy Kansas City - 1897-2017

Also by Randall L. O'Donnell
Nurturing Leadership

Science and heart:
The triumph of psychosocial care in pediatrics

Thomas McCormally
Randall L. O'Donnell

First edition

ISBN: 978-1-943338-18-4
Library of Congress Control Number: 2017939793

Published by Chandler Lake Books

Editor: Monroe Dodd
Book designer: Kelly Ludwig

Printed in the U.S.A.
by Walsworth Publishing, Marceline, Missouri

Contents

"Skill cannot take the place of sympathy and understanding, for science without heart is ugly and pitiless."

Katharine Berry Richardson, MD

Co-founder, Children's Mercy Kansas City

Psychosocial care

Psychosocial care is care that enhances the mental, social, spiritual, and emotional well-being of children, families and caregivers. It is care that is culturally sensitive and personalized. In pediatric settings, the primary responsibility for psychosocial care is with the departments of Child Life, Social Work and Chaplaincy, with nursing playing a significant role.

Patient- and Family-Centered Care

Patient- and family-centered care supports, respects, encourages and enhances the strengths and participation of patients and their families in their health care journey. It places an emphasis on partnerships among health care providers and people of all ages, at all levels of care, and in all health care settings. In children's health care it recognizes that the family is the constant in the child's life.

According to the Institute for Patient- and Family-Centered Care, this practice is based on the recognition that patients and families are essential allies, not only in direct care interactions, but also in quality improvement, safety initiatives, education of health professionals, research, facility design and policy development.

The core concepts of patient- and family-centered care:
- Dignity and respect
- Information sharing
- Participation
- Collaboration

The American Academy of Pediatrics in 2011 defined pediatric primary health care as "family centered and incorporates community resources and strengths, needs and risk factors, and sociocultural sensitivities into strategies for care delivery and clinical practice."

Foreword

A friend now living across the country told me the tragic story of her eight-year-old daughter's diagnosis with cancer. When the doctor disclosed the condition to her and her husband ("I regret to tell you Janie has cancer"), the words that followed from that doctor's lips were fully impalpable to my friend. Neither she nor her husband could hear anything but the echo of the word cancer. Not until they brought their daughter to Children's Mercy Kansas City did they understand the hospital's longstanding philosophy regarding the vital role a family plays in facilitating treatment and recovery. They would also come to appreciate the resources the hospital would dedicate to helping their daughter and family: medically, emotionally and socially.

At Children's Mercy, our doctors, nurses and other providers are unhesitating and proud when they tell the families of our patients, "We know more about health care than you do." But they are also quick and unhesitating to follow that with the expression of a humble truth: "You know more about your child than we do." This means the family is more than a spectator. Family is a true partner in the enterprise of treating the child.

Let me give you a couple of practical examples.

- When are you likely to see a chaplain at a hospital? Typically, it is when the health care crisis is so severe that the likelihood of survival is remote. But that's not the case at Children's Mercy. Here, within hours of a patient's admission to the hospital, a chaplain will call on the family to offer support, to become acquainted, to bring spiritual service in a secular manner so that even the family's intangible needs for a special kind of support are fulfilled from the very start.

- And what is the protocol if a child requires diagnostic tests, meaning blood will be drawn or big and loud machines will take pictures of the child's body? If those or any other complicated and sometimes intimidating steps are required, there will always be a Child Life professional at the patient's side – not only at the time of the test, but before it. The professional will talk about what is about to happen and will transform it from something that inspires fear or intimidation into something that is more of an adventure. The adventure will take place with support from a special friend who will form a close and trusting relationship with the child.

Are these adornments merely expensive and unnecessary? They are not. Psychosocial care represents far more than a fancy term to bring the aura of science to customer service. Although good customer service is essential to the successful operation of any enterprise these days, it is not the first step in the exercise of psychosocial care – not at all. Psychosocial care provides resources and health care treatments designed and directed to relieve children and families of the natural anxiety and psychological trauma that can arise from participation in a hospital experience.

In the pages of this book, you will learn how the principles of psychosocial care were practiced long before they enjoyed the sanction of science, and how those principles arose from solid research. The founders of Children's Mercy were two sisters, Alice Berry Graham and Katharine Berry Richardson, one a dentist and the other a surgeon. They brought the ideas of service above self and psychosocial care to our very first patient and left that kind of whole-child care as a legacy for the hospital they founded in 1897. That legacy defined our culture and is a source of pride and distinction for us to this very day.

You also will learn how psychosocial care has become more sophisticated, more calculated and more deliberately deployed, leading to better teamwork, better communication and better health outcomes.

Like all of medicine, the journey to provide the best psychosocial care is never-ending. Research continues to find the best ways to help children and their families lead better, healthier lives.

As former chair of the Children's Mercy Board of Directors and as an individual whose profession has been devoted to the principles that are practiced at Children's Mercy, I take great pride in respecting the sanctity of psychosocial care. Here it is not an afterthought but a first thought, just as it has been for more than 120 years.

Debbie Sosland-Edelman, PhD
May 2019

Debbie Sosland-Edelman, PhD, is Executive Director of the Sosland Foundation and a member and former chair of the Children's Mercy Board of Directors. She is a doctoral graduate in developmental and child psychology from the University of Kansas, where she researched the infants of adolescent mothers and for 12 years served as an adjunct professor in clinical pediatrics.

CHAPTER 1
....

The legacy

There is a lot to dislike about a hospital. Most people go there because they are sick or have suffered some traumatic experience or both. Inside, they face germs and needles and invasive tests and procedures. All around, there is pain and suffering.

For children, particularly ones under 4 years old, the experience can create lasting psychological effects. In the hospital, little ones meet a swirl of strangers — caregivers. However well-intentioned, these strangers bring odd-looking testing devices and medications and sometimes even do things that cause pain. In the hospital, machines small and large make strange and unending sounds. In the hospital, hardly anything smells like home. Stress becomes nearly unendurable.

But what if hospitals offered a kind of care that helps compensate for all the negatives? What if they had people who looked at every bit of the patient, including their whole lives and families?

What if they had people who built relationships and knew that well-being meant more than vital signs like blood pressure and temperature? What if they treated patients and their families as if life also went on *outside* the hospital walls, and understood that life could be far more complex and important than any single medical treatment?

Fortunately, there is a hospital that does just that.

Breaking the norm

Children's Mercy Kansas City has been, from its beginning in summer 1897, a different sort of hospital. It was founded by two sisters, Alice Berry Graham and Katharine Berry Richardson, one a dentist and the other a surgeon. The two broke social norms to establish their hospital and their legacy.

Growing up in Pennsylvania and Kentucky in the middle 1800s, the two learned the roots of hard work and service above self, and found their life's calling: helping others. They showed tenacity and drive wrapped in idealism — values said to have been instilled by their father, Stephen Payne Berry.

The sisters were undaunted by the male-dominated world of 19th-century medicine and set out on their own to create what became known in Kansas City as "The Hospital of the Little People."

They began by sponsoring a single bed in a women's and children's hospital that operated in a ramshackle old home next to railroad tracks in east Kansas City, Missouri. Just across the alley lay a brickyard. The place was noisy and dirty, and dust and smoke blew directly into patient rooms. Eventually, they would expand their operation and move it to larger, more suitable buildings.

Hospitals and medicine of the 1890s were crude by today's standards. Medicine itself had barely come out of the Dark Ages. Doctors knew little about germs, and the use of vaccines was in its infancy. Poor living conditions, inadequate nutrition and the generally unsanitary environment of cities posed a constant threat to public health.

Hospital care — if people could find it and afford it — was driven almost entirely by physicians. Patients, or their parents, had little say in their care, losing control to a nearly-complete stranger. Doctors had the knowledge and called the shots.

A century earlier, the doctor-patient relationships were different. In the 1700s, patients with comfortable incomes drove medical care. Doctors competed for them. According to a history of the doctor-patient relationship that appeared in 2007 in the *International Journal of Surgery*, patients came to doctors with their own complaints and self-diagnoses. Whether or not it was medically appropriate, doctors followed the patients' lead to keep the patients happy — and paying.

By the late 1700s, however, as hospitals emerged as places to treat non-wealthy patients, medical care and doctors became available to the masses. Doctors flexed their intellectual muscles and their medical knowledge to treat patients as they saw fit. Patients, now competing for doctors instead of the other way around, were expected to be docile, unquestioning and happy to accept the doctor's expertise.

The hospital became the cornerstone of medical care. Medical knowledge grew rapidly, and health care began to focus, according to the *International Journal of Surgery*, on "the accurate diagnosis of pathological lesions inside the body — the biomedical model of illness." This required the expert clinical and anatomical knowledge of a doctor. Patients were subjects, a collection of organs.

The paternalistic model of care resembled a parent-infant relationship, in which the infant depended wholly on the parent. The doctor's role, in this analogy, was to act in the patient's best medical interests. "Good patients" were considered those who submissively accepted the passive role of the infant.

This dominant-doctor/passive-patient model of care largely endured throughout the 19th and 20th centuries. It was into that mode that Drs. Graham and Richardson found themselves thrust as they began practicing dentistry and medicine in the 1880s. Yet perhaps because they were women in a male-dominated profession, or perhaps because of their upbringing, they saw things differently. They invited collaboration with other doctors and families and encouraged teamwork. The sisters took lessons they had learned early in life and translated them into a patient-centric model of care.

The sisters, and Katharine's husband James Ira Richardson, a merchant and later dentist, moved to Kansas City from Eau Claire, Wisconsin, in 1893. At the time, Kansas City was a booming and mostly filthy cowtown. The population had exploded from about 4,000 inhabitants 30 years earlier, when the Civil War ended, to 132,000 in the 1890 census.

Through most of that rapid growth, Kansas City cared little for making itself safe, clean or pretty. Its unpaved streets turned from dust in sunshine to muddy bogs after rain. Water in the Missouri and Kansas rivers grew putrid from open sewage. Scores of saloons operated alongside houses of prostitution among the stockyards, rail yards, grain elevators and warehouses of the city's West Bottoms.

Late 19th-century Kansas City was hardly a healthy place for children, but children there were, some brought by orphan trains. As a whole, society did not regard children highly. They were exploited for cheap labor and often suffered unimaginable neglect and abuse. For most, there was no one to take care of them if they were sick. In large part, children of that era were treated simply like little adults.

The cruder aspects of Kansas City in the 1890s might have been exactly what drew Drs. Graham and Richardson. The sisters had grown up believing it was their responsibility to care for those less fortunate and to make good citizens of their neighbors. Where was there a greater opportunity than a place teeming with poor laborers, poor sanitation and destitute children?

Their timing was good.

Working in the sisters' favor was what has become known as the Progressive Era in U.S. history. Born out of the economic and social problems brought by the Industrial Revolution, the Progressive movement of the time held that the problems facing society — poverty, violence and class antagonism among them — could best be addressed by providing a good environment, education and a safe workplace. Progressives also targeted the exploitation of children by various means such as child labor.

Also, some writers were beginning to suggest that children were different from adults. *The Century of the Child* by Ellen Key, a Swedish teacher and writer, was published in English in 1909. In it, Key argued that children's unique qualities demanded special attention. Another early child psychologist was John B. Watson, who wrote, *Psychological Care of Infant and Child* in 1928.

"No one today knows enough to raise a child," Watson wrote. "Radium has more scientific study put upon it in the last 15 years than has been given the first three years of infancy since the beginning of time."

More than medicine

Katharine Richardson believed that taking care of children meant more than just providing medical care. Children needed an education, so she and her sister opened a school at Children's Mercy. They needed spirituality so, to encourage support from all religious traditions, the hospital was opened to patients of all religions, and it remains that way today.

Replying to critics of free hospitals, she described the importance of a well-rounded childhood experience: "See if your argument applies to free school and free churches ... it takes the three to make a citizen."

Dr. Richardson had attended the Women's Medical College of Pennsylvania, a Quaker institution and one of the first medical schools in the country for women. It opened in 1850; she arrived three decades later, graduating in 1887. She studied pregnancy and childbirth and, instead of an optional fourth year of medical school, she spent three months at a maternal and infant clinic in New York operated by Dr. Elizabeth Blackwell, who in 1849 had become the first woman in the United States to receive a medical degree.

Even as a medical student and early in practice, Dr. Richardson challenged conventional wisdom. She firmly believed in hand-washing in an era when germ theory was relatively new, and she rejected the months of bed rest that were often prescribed by male doctors for pregnant women.

Pediatrics itself was a relatively recent specialty; the first children's hospital opened in 1855 in Philadelphia. By the time Children's Mercy opened 40 years later, it was the 23rd hospital just for children in the country. Children's Mercy was unique among those hospitals in its mission to accept patients regardless of address, religion or ability to pay.

Pediatrics as its own specialty continued to develop in the mid-19th century. German physician Abraham Jacobi is considered the father of American pediatrics. He received his medical training in Germany but later practiced in New York City and established the pediatrics chair at the New York Medical College in 1861. He was elected president of the American Pediatric Society, the first medical specialty society in the United States.

Dr. Jacobi was an early advocate of treating children not simply as "miniature men and women, with reduced doses and the same class of diseases in small bodies." He recognized the singular nature of taking care of children. Also, he believed that the pediatrician's role needed to extend beyond the hospital.

"It is not enough," he said in 1904, "to work at the individual bedside in the hospital. In the near or dim future, the pediatrician is to sit in and control school boards, health departments, legislatures. He is the legitimate advisory to the judge and the jury and a seat for the physician in the councils of the republic is what the people have a right to demand."

Dr. Charles C. Dennie, who trained at Children's Mercy as part of the Class of 1912 at the University of Kansas School of Medicine, described some of the medical challenges the sisters faced.

"The specialty of pediatrics was just emerging as a science, but not much had been accomplished along that line," he recalled in the 1960s in a series of articles about the history of Children's Mercy for the *Greater Kansas City Medical Bulletin*.

"When children were hospitalized in the 19th century," Dr. Dennie wrote, "they were placed in the same ward with adults where they were subject to cross infections. Feeding was primitive … year-old infants were fed corn and other rough food with the consequences that *cholera morbis* [a gastrointestinal illness], which is almost unknown today, was widespread and the mortality was great.

"If children developed various infections, they had to depend on their own defense mechanism and good nursing care to see them through. Typhoid fever … had a high mortality. Tetanus serum was used only as a preventive because if lockjaw had appeared the result was fatal.

"These were a few of the hazards that Dr. Richardson and Dr. Graham had to overcome."

And the sisters faced more challenges. As women, they were legally and socially second-class citizens, unable to vote and without much voice in the business world. They could not join their respective medical societies. They would need to form alliances with other women doctors and with the few businessmen and male doctors who were sympathetic to their cause.

Children's Mercy was incorporated on June 18, 1901, as the Free Bed Fund Association for Crippled, Deformed and Ruptured Children. (The word "sick" was added later and the official name changed to The Children's Mercy Hospital in 1919). Article 2 of the incorporation document showed that the sisters set their sights high, and well beyond traditional medicine:

"The object of this association and corporation shall be, by all lawful means, to aid in preventing neglect of and cruelty to crippled, deformed, ruptured and otherwise afflicted children; to assist children by surgical or medical means, or by nursing, also to promote the intellectual and temporal welfare of children under its care."

This was no patch-them-up, send-them-home sort of care. The sisters promoted whole-child care with the in-house school, with nurses filling the nurturing role of absent parents and with alternative treatments like massage and water therapy. They opened their own home where children could live temporarily so a hospital bed could be available to another child.

Nurses were included in the by-laws along with surgeons and other physicians. That demonstrated the value the founding sisters put in nurses and their ability to assist in the intellectual and worldly welfare of children. Katharine Richardson and Alice Graham understood that nurses spent more time with patients than did doctors and thus had a better chance to learn about the patients' families and understand their social conditions. They saw the world through different lenses than doctors. They had to.

Florence Nightingale, the founder of modern nursing, was also well known as a social reformer. In the middle 1800s, she saw the limits of traditional medicine and knew that care needed to extend beyond the operating room or the hospital. Best known for her care of wounded British soldiers during the Crimean War, Nightingale also focused some of her attention on the treatment of children and knew they required a special kind of care. She knew, long before it was popular, that children were not simply small adults.

"The causes of the enormous child mortality are perfectly well known," Nightingale wrote in her seminal 1860 book *Notes on Nursing: What it is and What it is Not*. "They are chiefly want of cleanliness, want of ventilation, want of whitewashing; in one word, defective household hygiene."

Children, she said, are more susceptible to noxious elements than adults and must receive greater protection. She encouraged the education of women — as the primary caregivers of children — as a way to keep children healthy.

Dr. Richardson admired Nightingale and greatly respected the role that nurses played. In fact, before Children's Mercy even had its own building, the sisters established a nursing school in 1901. Richardson is said to have sought out Nightingale for her approval of a design for the nursing caps bestowed by the Children's Mercy School of Nursing.

Nightingale said care for children often received little attention because it was believed their health was unmanageable.

"We are constantly told," she wrote, "'the circumstances which govern our children's health are beyond our control.' ... Not even mothers think it is worth their while to study them, to study how to give their children healthy existences."

Instead, Nightingale said, mothers left the matter up to doctors, saying it was "medical or physiological knowledge, fit only for doctors." But Nightingale countered that the logic was flawed:

"In watching diseases both in private houses and in public hospitals, the thing that strikes the experienced observer most forcibly is this: that the symptoms or the sufferings generally considered to be inevitable and incident to the disease are very often not symptoms of the disease at all, but of something quite different — of the want of fresh air, or of light or of warmth or of quiet or of cleanliness or of punctuality and care in the administration of diet, of each and all of these. ...

"If a patient is cold, if a patient is feverish, if a patient is faint, if he is sick after taking food, if he has a bed sore, it is generally the fault not of disease, but of the nursing.

"I use the word nursing for want of a better. It has been limited to signify little more than the administration of medicine and the application of poultices. It ought to signify the proper use of fresh air, light, warmth, cleanliness, quiet and the proper selection and administration of diet."

Nightingale saw that what patients needed was not simply medicine and hospitals. They needed nurses and other care providers who understood the environment in which patients lived. That was part of the early foundation of what in the 21st century became known as "social determinants of health." And for children that meant taking care of the whole child, not simply treating the symptoms of a disease.

Decades after Nightingale, a consensus grew among at least nurses that psychosocial issues such as a patient's environment and home life formed an important part of health care.

"All human activities are more or less interrelated," wrote Jessie L. Bearn, RN, in the *American Journal of Nursing* in 1917. "But probably one of the closest bonds is that between social and medical issues."

It could be argued that nurses were the original medical social workers and even the original Child Life professionals — although that term would not be invented until the 1960s. In today's world, Child Life staffers work to normalize the hospital environment for children and to relieve stress and anxiety for the children, their siblings and parents. Over the decades that role has come to be seen as vital in delivering high-quality care.

In her paper, Bearn said that both the nursing and social professions were "mediating agents" and required a mixture of physical and mental activity:

"A few qualities necessary for the success of either are: tact, humility, patience, enthusiasm ... readiness to shoulder responsibility, cool-headed action in emergency and tolerance toward religion, realizing the good in all and the human need for it in some form.

"We have already been taught about individual idiosyncrasies," she said of her fellow nurses, "and that each case is different and that diseases are more readily classified than humanity. So, also, we know the therapeutic value of hope.

"The seamy side of life has ceased to shock us. It is not a new experience to enter a disorganized home, often with family skeletons exposed and after securing the confidence and rendering personal service, to note unobtrusively but accurately the details which then help determine the diagnosis and prognosis. ..."

Further, she saw value in extending her care beyond pure medicine.

"As sickness draws out neighborly aid, so too will other troubles, and after asking help for the sick it becomes equally easy to solicit clothing, food and rent from the nearest natural sources."

Dr. Richardson, too, tried to stress the importance of her work with Children's Mercy as more than treating illness, but also treating what ailed society.

"Is it better to make a sick child self-supporting," she wrote in the hospital newsletter, "than to be taxed later for his care when he enters the poorhouse and becomes one of the great army of down-and-outs?"

Social work

Perhaps because she saw many children suffering from malnutrition, abuse and the effects of living in squalor, Dr. Richardson knew that she was battling more than disease and needed more than traditional medicine to fight that battle. Parents often dropped off their children at her hospital for extended periods of time — some for months or years — and nurses needed to assume the traditional roles of mothers and fathers. She raised funds to hire massage therapists, for instance, and she took patients into her home to help with their recovery after they no longer needed to be hospitalized and their own homes were not appropriate or available for convalescence. Children's Mercy opened the school within its walls in 1911 to encourage both a healthy mind and body. By the 1920s, Children's Mercy employed what today we call social workers. In those days, they were known as "out workers."

Medical social work originated in England. The first social work service was formally established at St. Thomas' Hospital in London in 1909, according to *The Social Worker Speaks: A History of Social Workers through the Twentieth Century*. In the United States, Massachusetts General Hospital was the first to have professional social workers on site.

In 1905, Ida Maud Cannon went to work for Dr. Richard Cabot at Massachusetts General, having graduated from the Boston School for Social Work. Her goal was "to make medical care effective," according to the National Association of Social Work Foundation. In 1915, she was named "Chief of Social Service," establishing the first organized social work department in a hospital.

Begun in the outpatient clinics, Social Service focused on patients with tuberculosis, a major health problem of the era, along with neurological problems, venereal disease, unmarried pregnant girls and children with orthopedic problems. In 1918, Cannon founded the American Association of Hospital Social Workers.

The "out workers" at Children's Mercy made home visits and kept track of sociological data, in line with Cannon's charge "to make medical care effective." The hospital shared out workers' reports with the staff and the public and often included information outside the normal concerns of "medicine" or "hospitals." Katharine Richardson, a firm supporter of the Prohibition of alcohol in the 1920s, wrote that "Out workers reported that more than two-thirds of poverty and cruelty in the homes they visited were caused by drink."

The August 1931 issue of the Mercy *Messenger*, a monthly newsletter edited by the founding sisters to share information and solicit funds, included a report from out worker Mary Ryan. Her observations showed the effects of the Roaring '20s and the Great Depression. Among her comments:

- *Until recently – increasing evidence of prosperity in homes*
- *Increasing demand for help*
- *Better looking class of people in clinics*
- *Marked embarrassment at necessity of asking assistance*
- *Fathers coming to clinics with children*
- *Disappearance from home of furniture, radios, rugs, cars, etc.*
- *Great anxiety about jobs.*

I find great need of warm clothing for the children and overcoats for men and will be glad to distribute any such garments sent to Mercy Hospital.

At the same time that Children's Mercy was establishing itself as an advocate for children in Kansas City, two complementary social phenomena were at work: increased attention to the needs and care of children, and the exploration of new, alternative, forms of medicine.

Without government support for health care, such as Medicaid or Social Security, Dr. Graham and Dr. Richardson spent much of their time soliciting contributions of money, bedding and food. Fortunately for their cause, society's views on the treatment and welfare of children were changing.

In early 1909, President Theodore Roosevelt convened a group of medical professionals and lay leaders for the first White House Conference on the Care of Dependent Children. This helped bring a national focus to the health and well-being of children and provided an avenue for government leadership in childhood diseases, infant mortality and child-labor laws. The conference led to the development of the Children's Bureau under Roosevelt's successor, William Howard Taft, in 1912. The mission of the bureau was to "investigate and report upon matters pertaining to the welfare of children and child life among all classes of people."

Federal involvement was controversial, and cries of socialism came loud and clear. It also was controversial when Julia C. Lathrop, a social reformer from Illinois, was appointed to lead the new Children's Bureau. She was the first woman selected to lead a federal statutory agency. Clearly, national attention was being drawn to the kind of work being done at Children's Mercy and elsewhere.

President Woodrow Wilson, who succeeded Taft, announced the Baby Week Campaign in 1917, saying, "Next to the duty of doing everything possible for the soldiers at the front, there could be, it seems to me, no more patriotic duty than that of protecting the children who constitute one-third of our population." Baby Week helped lead to increased awareness of maternal and child health issues among state and local health agencies.

And as society began to view children through a different lens, medicine, too, began to change. In her early years as a physician, Katharine Richardson earned a reputation as an innovator. In the 1880s she had become an advocate for cleanliness, which from a 21st-century perspective seems only common sense. In the 19th century, however, the germ theory of the spread of disease was "new medicine." In fact, according to an American Academy of Pediatrics article, cleanliness was "looked upon as a modern fetish in those times." Some doctors scoffed at the notion of washing hands before operating. Dr. Richardson sided with those who promoted sanitation. (She did not, however, wear gloves to perform surgery.)

Long before widespread adoption of alternative medicine, its innovations were being practiced at Children's Mercy. Dr. Richardson sent one of her staff members to the French Alps to study under Dr. Auguste Rollier, who first documented the benefits of ultraviolet rays.

"All progressive hospitals, as well as all progressive physicians (are studying) the curative action of the sun," declared the hospital's 1927 School of Nursing brochure. The rooftop of the hospital's building on Independence Avenue contained a "sun cure porch."

In the 1890s, three new systems of alternative or "complementary" medicine opened schools and began to send graduates into practice. Osteopathy, naturopathy and chiropractic all came into practice at a time of growing mistrust of traditional medicine. In 1910, a report commissioned by the Carnegie Foundation found that while there was an abundance (or overabundance) of medical schools, there was often no formal curriculum, no prerequisite academic preparation and no mandatory written exams. The report's author, Abraham Flexner, proposed a four-year medical school, two of basic science and two of clinical training. The report resulted in the closure of many medical schools that were not part of a university.

By the 1920s, surveys showed that 25 to 75 percent of the American population received treatments from so-called "drugless healers" at least occasionally. These "new" forms of medical practice shared some things:

- Osteopathic physicians worked in partnership with patients and focused on health education, injury prevention and disease prevention. They emphasized medical care that promoted the body's ability to heal itself and consider the impact of lifestyle and community on health.
- Naturopathy emphasized prevention, treatment and health through therapy and substances that encouraged inherent self-healing. The physicians educated their patients, encouraged self-responsibility for health and took into account individual physical, mental, emotional, genetic, environmental, social and other factors.
- Chiropractic focused on the relationship between the body's structure and its functioning, supporting the body's natural ability to heal itself.

And there were others, all seeking new, better, different ways to care for patients.

Some scoffed at the methodologies of some of these alternative practices, but Dr. Richardson was not beyond trying anything reasonable to help her patients. Children's Mercy was among the first children's hospitals to offer massage, along with water therapy, a gymnasium and a playground. When the hospital opened its own public school — it was only the second school in the country to operate inside a hospital — it testified to the belief that a strong body and a strong mind were both important to health and health care.

One report at the time described the care this way: "Science and skill and child love have triumphed."

Children's Mercy was established and operated by its founders for 36 years (Dr. Graham died in 1913 and Dr. Richardson in 1933) as an innovative hospital, not afraid to break the norm. It took only poor children and it took them regardless of their address or their background. The sisters knew its work extended beyond the walls of the hospital and beyond the boundaries of traditional medicine.

Their foundation of caring for children had been firmly established and would endure. Despite financial, leadership and other challenges during the Great Depression and World War II, Children's Mercy looked after its children in a way no ordinary hospital would, or could.

And more changes were on the way, in both society and in health care. By the middle of the 20th century, many aspects of child care, parenting and medicine were being studied and new approaches were being considered.

Children's Mercy, with solid principles and practices of caring for all children — and in every way possible — would be there.

CHAPTER 2

....

Humanitarian and scientific foundation

By the middle of the 20th century, a period some dubbed the Century of the Child, American society began to take a different approach to children, how to raise them and how to care for them. The post-World War II Baby Boom made it impossible to ignore the needs of children and their impact on families and communities.

New approaches to child-rearing and health care, especially mental health, surfaced. What followed in the 1950s, '60s and '70s was new science, new psychology and new models of parenting.

The medical professions, although not always quick to adapt, found it hard to ignore new theories about development and child-rearing and a growing library of research about the impact of hospitalization and medical treatment on growing children.

A new profession, Child Life, emerged in the 1950s and its practitioners gradually began working alongside doctors, nurses, social workers and chaplains. The foundation was being laid for the growing field of psychosocial care — care for the total child.

Man as machine

Before the mid-1900s, the leading parenting philosophy was one articulated by J.B. Watson, whom some consider the founder of the science of behaviorism. Watson, in his 1928 book, *Psychological Care of Infant and Child*, pushed the notion of "man as machine," of human beings as physical substances that should perform as expected. For Watson, happiness consisted of being self-reliant, productive and devoid of emotion. He had little concern for the social nature of children.

"Treat them as though they are small adults," Watson wrote. "Never hug them and kiss them, never let them sit on your lap. If you must, kiss them once on the forehead when they say goodnight. Shake hands with them in the morning. Give them a pat on the head if they have made an extraordinarily good job of a difficult task. Try it out. In a week's time, you will find how easy it is to be perfectly objective with your child and at the same time, kindly. You will be utterly ashamed of the mawkish, sentimental way you have been handling it."

His philosophy gained widespread acceptance. *The New York Times* heralded him as a groundbreaking scientist.

After World War II, along came a German psychologist with a different approach. Erik Erikson was the first to popularize the phrase "psychosocial development" in 1959 to describe how children were not purely biological organisms — and certainly not machines — but additionally the product of the world around them.

Today, the psychosocial approach to pediatric health care views children as the result of the combined influences of their psychological states and their social environment, of both nature and nurture. The best pediatric caregivers understand how psychosocial factors influence physical and mental health, as well as the ability to function in society.

Erikson is best known for his eight psychosocial stages of development, which cover the human lifespan. He theorized that each stage of life was associated with predictable psychological struggles that contribute to a major aspect of personality.

Erikson's stages of psychosocial development

- Hope: Trust vs. Mistrust (Oral-sensory, infancy, 0-2 years)
- Will: Autonomy vs.Shame/Doubt (early childhood, 2-4 years)
- Purpose: Initiative vs. Guilt (locomotor-genital, pre-school, 4-5 years)
- Competence: Industry vs. Inferiority (latency, school age, 5-12 years)
- Fidelity: Identity vs. Role confusion (adolescence, 13-19 years)
- Love: Intimacy vs. Isolation (early adulthood 20-39 years)
- Care: Generativity vs. Stagnation (adulthood 40-64 years)
- Wisdom: Ego integrity vs. Despair (maturity 65-death)

In each stage, Erikson said, certain personality traits develop that help guide a person through the rest of life. In the first years of life, children learn trust (or mistrust), autonomy (or doubt), initiative (or guilt.) Adolescents, building on the earlier phases, discover their identity (or not). Young adults discover intimacy or isolation.

According to Erikson, each phase must be successfully navigated to pave the way for later health, both mental and physical. Experts have come to believe that, by understanding these phases, health care professionals can design and provide optimum care, communication and education.

Consider Erikson's earliest two stages of development, from birth to age 4. First comes infancy, in which the primary question is trust vs. mistrust. If the infant learns to trust the world and the people around him or her, the resulting virtue is hope. Then comes the toddler stage. Toddlers deal with autonomy, learning to do things on their own, and if they succeed will gain the virtue of will. These virtues the child will carry for the rest of life. Hope, for instance, not only is important to good mental health and a positive attitude, but also is linked to physical health: A life without hope easily can lead to bad choices, such as lawlessness and drug or alcohol abuse, with dire health consequences.

According to Erikson, a person develops as he or she successfully resolves crises that are distinctly social in nature. Besides establishing a sense of trust in others, this entails developing a sense of identity in society and, later in life, understanding and living in love and helping the next generation prepare for the future. He described this lifetime of development as "psychosocial" because it involved the psychological needs of the individual in concert or conflict with the needs of society.

By emphasizing the role of culture and society, Erikson's work stood as particularly significant viewed against the work of Sigmund Freud and others who believed the conflicts that led to psychological development were all internal.

The Erikson Institute, a Chicago-based school of higher education for those who work with children, says one of its namesake's lasting contributions has been placing children squarely in the context of society. The institute states that he "advanced the idea that children are not simply biological organizations that endure, nor products of the psyche in isolation. Rather, they develop in the context of society's expectations, prejudices and prohibitions."

Erikson's work built on the developmental stage theory of Swiss psychologist Jean Piaget. Piaget's theory centers on the phases children go through as they explore the world around them, learn to pretend, begin to think logically and concretely and finally discover abstract thought and knowledge. Today's child-care

Piaget's stages of development

- Sensorimotor (0-2 years): The infant explores the world through direct sensory and motor contacts. Object permanence and separation anxiety develop during this stage.
- Preoperational (2-6 years): The child uses symbols — words and images — to represent objects, but does not reason logically. The child also has the ability to pretend. During this stage, the child is egocentric.
- Concrete operational (7-12 years): The child can think logically about concrete objects and can thus add and subtract. The child also understands conservation.
- Formal operational (12 years – adult): The adolescent can reason abstractly and think in hypothetical terms.

workers use these phases to help guide their interactions with children, based on their ability to understand and communicate.

At the same time that Erikson's views were taking hold in the middle 20th century, new theories of parenting were also being introduced. These new views would further challenge society's approach to children.

Leading the way was Dr. Benjamin Spock and his book, *The Common Sense Book of Baby and Child Care*. Dr. Spock departed drastically from Watson's view of babies as little machines, instead encouraging parents to go with their instincts.

"Trust yourself. You know more than you think you do," were the opening words of the first edition of his book, published in 1946, right in time for the Baby Boom.

According to *The New York Times Magazine* in 1999, pediatricians in the 1930s and '40s had found themselves "confounded and annoyed by the large number of distraught, angry and frazzled mothers" who complained they could not abide by the strict schedules and purely objective training proposed by Watson and the equally "hoary" classic, *The Care and Feeding of Children*, by Luther Emmett Holt.

By the late 1940s, "Watsons had begun to give way to the child-centered, Spock-espoused approach that would have us, say, walk our colicky babies for hours in the middle of the night rather than let them cry it out, or painstakingly 'kid-proof' our houses rather that swat a toddler who menaces the porcelain."

Working on his residency in the early 1930s in New York, Dr. Spock came to believe that pediatricians should study psychology, a rather radical thought at a time when mental and physical health were considered drastically distinct propositions.

Dr. Spock's philosophy, although popular enough to sell about 50 million copies of his book in more than 40 languages, was not without its detractors. Critics warned that Dr. Spock was too permissive and that coddling babies and children would eventually make them self-indulgent and rebellious. This view took on added emphasis in the 1960s when many Baby Boomers protested the Vietnam War and took to the streets for other social causes. (Dr. Spock himself joined some of those protests and was arrested for civil disobedience.)

Perhaps the one idea he stressed that took root most firmly echoed a theme of many innovative pediatricians and others concerned with child health: that children are unique individuals and not just small adults. *TIME* magazine in 2011 included an article marking the 65th anniversary of the publication of *Baby and Child Care*. It was called "Five Ideas that Changed American Parenting." Number Five was: "Babies need love."

"It seems almost ludicrous today that anyone could ever think otherwise. But this idea was by no means taken for granted just 100 years ago. Early 20th-century child-rearing guides warned parents not to kiss their babies or cradle them too much, lest the children become spoiled.

"Spock taught his readers that babies were little people with their own emotional needs and that they should be cherished, not encouraged to meet the schedules and rules of adult life as quickly as possible."

The latest edition of *Baby and Child Care* says: "Children are driven from within themselves to grow, explore, experience, learn and build relationships with other people. So while trusting yourself, remember to also trust your child."

Among those who followed Dr. Spock in the child-centered parenting-advice arena was Dr. T. Berry Brazelton. *The New York Times* called him the most celebrated baby doctor since Spock and said that Brazelton revolutionized our understanding of how children developed psychologically.

After his training in pediatrics at Children's Hospital of Boston, Dr. Brazelton went on to study child psychiatry at Massachusetts General. He did not believe that his pediatric training, rich in rare diseases and vaccine schedules, allowed him to get to really know patients. Dr. Brazelton was among the first who realized that newborns were complex, responsive and competent at birth. He used videotape to research mother-baby interaction. He was able to show that babies had the ability to engage, or disengage, according to what was going on around them.

"The notion of mother-infant bonding, now gospel among early-childhood experts, grew out of this research," *The Times* said in its obituary of Dr. Brazelton in 2018.

Dr. Brazelton popularized the notion of meeting children "where they're at," a phrase that meant a child's needs depended on a variety of factors, psychological, social and medical. That phrase is common at hospitals that practice psychosocial care. Brazelton emphasized the unique nature of children, their home life, parents, siblings and the rest of their environment. By sitting on the floor with children, he engaged them physically at their own level. Likewise, he talked with them in appropriate language to connect emotionally.

"He astonished us by concentrating on a topic important to parents that had otherwise been neglected in our residency," Dr. Perri Klass wrote in 2018 about her time as a resident under Dr. Brazelton. "He asked us what we knew about toilet training, and its problems, and he told us about his patients and what he had learned from them."

Rounding out a triumvirate of child-rearing leaders who shaped the view of children and their development was Dr. Penelope Leach, who wrote *Your Baby and Child: From Birth to Age Five*, first published in 1978.

Dr. Leach liked to point out that of the three — Drs. Spock, Brazelton and her — she was the only woman and the only one who knew precisely what it meant to be a mother. She urged mothers to take a year or more off work to give their babies a proper start in life. She also told mothers, "Only you really know your baby," and suggested they form a partnership with doctors, each providing their own expertise.

This was an important teaching for advocates of family-centered care. Doctors have medical expertise, yet parents know their children the way doctors never will. Together, they can become a powerful force in treating and caring for children.

Building on the work of those who came before her, Dr. Leach stressed the importance of comforting children.

"The happier you can make your baby," she said, "the more you will enjoy being with her and the more you enjoy her, the happier she will be."

By the 2000s, science was beginning to validate some of Leach's philosophies. Neuroscientists have shown that babies with uncontrolled crying have sky-high levels of the stress hormone cortisol. Because a baby's brain is still in development, too much cortisol can be damaging.

"What you are doing at this stage," Dr. Leach wrote in *The Independent* magazine in 2010, "is sculpting the connections in the brain. When someone comes and comforts the baby, the cortisol (produced when the baby cries) gives place to the happy hormones, endorphins, which flood in instead. So, over time, if the baby is almost always picked up and comforted, then the connections in the brain will teach it that when stress hormones flood the brain, endorphins kick in. Eventually, you reach the point where stress corrects itself and that's what we talk about self-soothing."

A flurry of scientific research on the effects of medical care and hospitalization on children continued to push the medical professions toward a new thinking and new way of operating to provide the best possible care for children. But progress did not come quickly.

The "best" care for kids

Medical science made astounding progress in the 1900s. Life expectancy increased by at least 50 percent, depending on race and sex. Infant mortality — the number of babies who die before their first birthday — showed an even more incredible improvement, from about 100 for every 1,000 births in 1900 to just over 7 per 1,000 before the year 2000.

In pediatrics, much attention had been paid to infectious disease and nutrition. The results, obviously, were encouraging. New treatments, new medications such as vaccines and new equipment were making health care more effective and giving children chances for healthier, longer lives.

Perhaps because of that progress, the last half of the century was marked by a shift in pediatrics toward the study of behavioral and social aspects of children's health. A plethora of studies published in scientific journals and elsewhere attested to the emotional benefits and drawbacks of certain medical practices. That work helped further the notion of psychosocial care for children and their families.

The book *Psychosocial Research on Pediatric Hospitalization and Health Care* by Richard Thompson, PhD, is filled with examples from scientific literature about how care for children affects them. Far from focusing solely on psychological impact, the book includes research that shows how psychosocial care can reduce physical symptoms — high blood pressure and increased heart rate, for example — and improve recuperation.

Anna Freud, a psychologist and youngest daughter of psychoanalyst Sigmund Freud, wrote in 1952 that the care of children had become fragmented through specialization and that parents were essential to providing the best possible care for their children. This was at a time when parents still were routinely dismissed by doctors and nurses as important to the care of their children.

In her book, *The Psychoanalytic Study of the Child*, Freud wrote that care had to be taken so that the treatment of the child did not cause more damage than the ailment for which the child was being treated.

"The child is unable to distinguish between feelings of suffering caused by the disease inside the body and suffering imposed on him from outside for the sake of curing the disease," Freud wrote. "He has to submit uncomprehendingly, helplessly and passively to both sets of experiences."

That would serve as an early foundation for work designed to give children under treatment as great a feeling of control as possible.

Freud also documented physical reaction to psychological stresses such as sore throats, upset stomachs and increased temperatures. Although inflicting some pain may be unavoidable, she said, health care workers should strive to reduce anxiety to avoid the "trauma of pain." Her study was perhaps the first to show the negative physical effects of hospitalization on children.

Hospitalization can cause a variety of negative reactions in children: uncontrollable crying, anxiety, aggressive behavior, bedwetting. In some cases, the children return to normal shortly after returning home. But there is also evidence that some children have significant difficulties for a long time afterward. One study from 1957 showed that, for children under age 4, hospitalization for as little as five days could make them "emotionally disturbed" for at least six months after discharge.

Even more evidence showed the link between emotional stress and physical harm.

"The hospital, aided and abetted by the cult of asepsis, the increased efficiency of time and motion theory and the depersonalization of automation has been progressing toward a total isolation of the child from his previous emotional contacts, which are based on familiar human beings and objects," wrote R. F. Briggs, MD, in *Hospital Management* in 1967. "There comes a point, difficult to determine in this continuum of emotional deprivation, where the child's body becomes less able to promote healing and resist infection."

Depending where the child is in Erikson's stages of development, isolation and a violation of trust or autonomy could result in psychological setbacks that could affect the child well into the future.

The push toward a child-centered care approach extended beyond the medical community. *The Annals* of the American Academy of Political Science found the mounting evidence hard to ignore. In 1963, it published "Meeting Patients' Psychosocial Needs in the General Hospital." The article said:

"As psychosocial factors become increasingly recognized as determinants of therapeutic progress, the need becomes clearer for hospitals, physicians and nurses to consider the psychosocial and cultural needs of patients and treat the whole person and not merely a disease entity.

"Many patients enter the hospital with anxiety not only about physical condition, but also about family, occupational and financial matters. They hope to find

Hospitals as a health hazard for children

"Hospitalization is usually viewed by society as a health aid; however, few realize the health hazard that the hospital presents to the emotional life of the infant or young child."

Those are the opening words of "The Hospitalized Child Faces Emotional Hazards" by R.F. Briggs, MD, in the May 1967 edition of *Hospital Management.* In a review of literature on the subject, Briggs listed some of the things that influenced the outcome of hospitalization:

- Age of the child.
- Level of satisfaction of relationships with the mother before hospitalization.
- Length of hospitalization.
- Amount of contact (quantity and quality) with the mother while in the hospital.
- Amount of contact with other familiar persons — father, grandparents, siblings — and familiar objects — favorite toys — while in the hospital.
- Amount of substitute *mothering* in the hospital.
- Ability to comprehend what is happening and why.
- Amount of preparation for hospital and for specific procedures.
- Parents' ability to understand and cope with post-hospital upset.

technical skill, sympathetic understanding and an agreeable physical and social environment."

A Boston Children's study looked at practices such as educational preparation for children and parents before procedures. The study found that children were able to master their anxieties by acting out in play or by talking about their fantasies or feelings of fear. In addition, this work shone a spotlight on the importance of age-appropriate communication with children, depending on their stage of development. For example:

- A 3-year-old was worried that blood would be taken out and tomato juice put back in.
- A 9-year-old exhibited high anxiety that his leg would be amputated because his mom told him if he did not cooperate with treatment the doctors would cut it off.
- Many children interpreted their illness as "magical retribution," saying, "God makes you sick because you're bad" or "I think it was something I did."

By knowing where children fit in the Erikson stages of development, appropriate education, communication and treatment can be prescribed.

The question of visitation

Among the approaches to care being studied as early as the late 1940s was expanded visitation for parents and other family members. In some instances parents, usually mothers, were "admitted" to the hospital along with their children. That was particularly popular in other countries, but was not widely adopted in the United States.

Some critics suggested that parental visitation only upset children, who were then forced to bear repeated separations. Some hospitals kept parents out because doctors and nurses worried they would get in the way, tell them how to do their jobs or otherwise interfere with treatment.

In 1956, Henry H. Work, MD, wrote "Making Hospitalization Easier for Children" in the journal *Children*. In some New York hospitals, he noted, parental visitation resulted in positive side effects. One, he said, occurred in teaching hospitals, where residents and students got to observe family dynamics and to develop "a much broader concept of pediatric practice." In years to come, that concept would take on the name "family-centered care."

Boston Floating Hospital (so named because it was established in 1894 on a ship in Boston Harbor) was one of the early adopters of expanded visitation. In 1949, the hospital began to accept some mothers as "residents" of the hospital along with their inpatient children. Dr. Veronica Tisza in 1956 explained the reaction:

"The staff's close contact with parents has led to an empathy with their grief and anxieties and has replaced the former identification with the child with a family orientation. A change in attitudes, motivated by the acceptance of the concept of the 'total care of the child' has occurred gradually."

In Great Britain, a film by James Robertson, "A Two-Year-Old Goes to the Hospital," was released in 1952. According to a report in *Children* by Ann Hales Tooke, the movie "exploded" the belief that a child who was quiet in the hospital was "settled."

"The film clearly shows what Mr. Robertson called the three phases of response to separation: protest, despair and detachment," Tooke wrote.

That film was followed by another in 1958, "Going to the Hospital with Mother," which showed the benefits of admitting mothers to hospitals with their small children. The two documentaries resulted in two major recommendations in Great Britain: parents should be able to visit their children at any reasonable time of day, and, where possible, mothers should be admitted with their hospitalized preschoolers.

Involving parents directly in hospital care might have seemed radical in the United States, but in so-called developing countries of Africa and Asia the family was a vital part of the equation. A study from the journal *Children* of 150 countries in the mid-1960s found widespread adoption of family involvement.

"We found all levels of care and treatment for children," wrote authors John E. Bell and Elisabeth A. Bell. "But no matter what the level of medical care, we found nearly everywhere that the child had the security of the immediate love and care of his mother or other relatives 24 hours every day."

The Bells noted there was some suspicion among hospital staff of family involvement, including worries about infection control and parental interference. In some cases, doctors made their rounds when parents were sure to be at the bedside; in other cases, doctors preferred that parents be absent. They also wrote that problems sometimes arose where nurses and mothers saw each other as competitors instead of partners.

But the study concluded that the benefits far outweighed any complications.

"Overworked staff members are able to use their time for professional functions; money can be spent for drugs and treatment instead of basic domestic provisions; and the quality of care is raised.

"Participation of the family in hospital care is not an exotic curiosity, but a natural expression of family conviction, strongly adhered to in three-fourths of the world. The practice is followed because it is a humane response to the rights of children. We believe that access to the best in health care is a right for all children. In our minds it follows that family access to children in hospitals is equally a right."

Almost as soon as Children's Mercy moved to its new home on Hospital Hill in Kansas City in 1970, the same year the Bell study was published, plans were made to add a Parent Care Unit, designed for children who needed hospitalization but not acute, critical care. Parents stayed 24 hours a day and even administered medication and checked vital signs such as pulse, blood pressure and temperature — with supervision.

An article about the unit appeared in the American Medical Association's publication, *Medical News:*

"The facility ... encourages close parent-child relationships during a stressful period." It also reduced cost, which was something also reported by Boston Floating Hospital more than a decade earlier.

Another advantage of parental involvement was suggested in a 1968 study that considered stress on children and their parents. In "Children, Stress and Hospitalization: A Field Experiment," the authors noted that communication was a key to reducing parental stress. When hospital staff interacted with mothers, providing both information and emotional support, a mom's stress was lowered.

"This, in turn, may reduce a child's stress," the study said, "and have profound effect on his social, psychological and even physiological response to hospitalization and surgery."

The study further noted that illness affected the whole family, not only the sick child, and that the negative experiences of hospitalization "may even lead to grave psychological problems years after the child has been discharged."

Researchers James K. Skipper Jr. from Case Western Reserve University and Robert C. Leonard from the University of Arizona said the social environment of the hospital could result in higher body temperature, pulse rate and blood pressure, post-operative vomiting, disturbed sleep and longer recovery period. They recommended parental involvement and special attention to a child's psychosocial adjustment.

Despite all this evidence, the health care establishment proved slow to adopt widespread changes in how children's special needs were treated. Decades after research began to show the harmful effects of hospitalization, a study from 1970 pressured the health care establishment to make changes in light of an abundance of evidence.

"Nearly two decades ago the pediatric literature was filled with reports concerning the psychological damage hospitalization can do to a child," T.P. Millar wrote in *Children.*

He recalled one study that found 92 percent of children showed "significant disturbances in behavior not present prior to hospitalization." Further, he said that for children under the age of 4 the threat of lasting damage was great. Echoing the work of Erik Erikson, Millar noted the giant steps in psychological growth during the pre-school years.

"At this busiest of times, the child cannot divert its energies to dealing with an overwhelming emotional experience and still achieve this complex psychological growth at a normal rate," he said. "Therefore, even brief hospitalization carries with it significant psychological hazard."

Millar described some of the ways a hospital visit and overnight stay could confuse and confound a child:

"Hospitalizing the preschool child violates [the developmental] process. The degree of separation is usually beyond the adaptive capacity of the child. ... The child is at the same time subjected to other stresses. He is likely to be in pain, which may well be the worst feeling he has ever known and his mother, who usually takes away unpleasant feelings, is not there to help him.

"He is surrounded by strange people whose clothes are all alike, but whose faces are somehow different — people who stay awhile and then go away. Sometimes they return. Sometimes they do not. Some of them wear masks like bad guys on TV. They smile, then do things that hurt. There are giant machines that tilt and whir and descend on you. Things smell funny. Any hour of the day or night, somewhere children are crying.

"For the child under 4 years of age, the hospital is a strange and frightening world, and he is alone in it."

As medical science advanced, pediatrics became increasingly specialized. The role of the family doctor was being replaced by specialists. The share of all doctors reporting themselves as full-time specialists increased from 55 percent in 1960 to 69 percent in 1970.

Specialization brought fragmentation of care and challenges to communication and to familiarity among medical disciplines, nurses, other health professionals, parents and children. As medical centers themselves grew physically and operationally, so did the bureaucracy that was built around doctors and hospital staff, often at the expense of a network that supported families.

There had to be a better way.

A new discipline emerges

Widespread adoption of a psychosocial approach to health care was — and is — a long, slow trudge, but there were pioneers stretching back to the early decades of the 20th century.

Even before Piaget and Erikson and the studies that looked at the hazards of medical care, some hospitals adopted a child-friendly approach. C.S. Mott Children's Hospital at the University of Michigan established an early play program for children in 1922.

The Association of Child Life Professionals calls the Mott program the beginning of their discipline. Child Life is the profession of specialists who help children and families cope with illness, trauma, disability and loss. They provide ways through play, preparation and education to reduce fear, anxiety and pain.

Children's Mercy, too, provided play opportunities for children in the 1920s, in part through its Junior League Play Room. The hospital also had a playground on the grounds of the hospital, then situated on Independence Avenue in northeast Kansas City, Missouri.

Other hospitals began to add play programs to address some of the emotional and developmental needs of children and by the 1950s there were at least nine organized play programs at North American children's hospitals.

The field of Child Life began to take off in the 1950s when an Austrian child development specialist opened a Child Life and Education Division at the Cleveland City Hospital. The specialist, Emma Plank, studied in Vienna under Maria Montessori and Anna Freud before coming to the United States in 1938. She was invited in 1955 to join the Department of Pediatrics at City Hospital by Dr. Frederick C. Robbins "to address the educational, social and psychological needs of children receiving long-term care."

In 1962, Plank published what has become the classic textbook of the child life profession, *Working with Children in Hospitals*. The foreword set the stage for this sprouting field of work:

"Doctors are more specialized and often the physicians caring for a child in the hospital are not involved with his longer term overall care. ... With the shortage of nurses, and the increased demand on their time, they are less able to concern themselves with the emotional needs of the patients. Thus, it is possible for the hospital situation to become excessively impersonal with a great deal of attention paid to the child's illness and too little to his feelings. ...

"Someone must defend the child against the system," Plank said. "It is as the child's advocate against the system that the child-care worker fulfills her most important role.

"When an adult is hospitalized, his normal way of living and activity is interrupted. He can resume the cycle when his health is restored. Children cannot do this. The growing child cannot afford to interrupt the cycle of his living and growth. When a child is hospitalized, the hospital has to take on tasks beyond its healing function, tasks which must be accomplished so the rhythm of life and growth can go on."

Plank and her supporters would position the child life professional, earlier known as a child-care worker, right in the middle of the health care team. It was not always an easy fit; doctors and nurses were — and some still are — confused about roles or unconvinced of their need.

But as more people began to see the value of Child Life, and as evidence mounted that care of children required more than attention to their medical needs, other hospitals began to adopt programs to address psychosocial questions.

In 1965, Plank and others formed what became the Association for the Care of Children's Health. At its second conference, representatives from pediatrics, surgery, nursing and social work joined the discussions with Child Life professionals. And by the third meeting, more potential participants applied than could be accommodated. By 1975, the association drew members from 45 states, Canada and several other countries. The number of Child Life programs grew from 10 in 1950 to 170 twenty-five years later.

The association eventually dissolved as the separate disciplines grew larger and formed their own associations. But the vitality of psychosocial services had been established.

A related movement in medicine was also gaining steam: the drive for a patient-centered model of care.

Too often, critics claimed, hospitals and medical clinics were designed and functioned solely for the benefit of doctors and other health care providers: limited visiting hours, appointments only during the week and during normal day-time working hours and no accommodations for siblings or extended family. Hospitals were fraught with poor communication and poor coordination and the needs of the patients and families were often secondary.

"The modern hospital is a notoriously poor organization for eliciting information, providing support or generating a reassuring atmosphere," Skipper and Leonard wrote in their 1968 study on stress in children and families. "The lack of information and lack of emotional warmth from physicians and nurses are among the most criticized aspects of patient care."

But at the Association for the Care of Children's Health and other organizations, the needs of patients were taking center stage. In England, Enid and Michael Balint did groundbreaking work. In a lecture entitled "The Possibilities of Patient-centered Medicine" in 1969, the Balints suggested it was time to expand on illness-centered medicine.

"There is another way of medical thinking which we call 'patient centered medicine,'" Enid said. "Here, in addition to trying to discover a localized illness or illnesses, the doctor also has to examine the whole person in order to form what we call an 'overall diagnosis.'"

The idea was rejected by many in the medical profession in part because they worried it would take too much time. Yet the Balints' research showed that getting to know patients actually took little additional time.

Others worried that medical doctors were not trained in psychotherapy, and had only limited understanding of mental illness or its treatments. Patient-centered medicine might uncover issues for which they had no answers. That is one reason mental health questions still are not addressed in many doctors' offices.

Nevertheless, all this work helped define the role of the Child Life specialist and others to support doctors and the rest of the traditional medical team. As medicine became ever more specialized, and as evidence mounted that the whole family and society played a role in child health, it began to make sense to include professionals in child development and social work.

The ground was being prepared for the acceptance of a broader role for psychosocial care. But it did not happen overnight.

Tenacious and idealistic, the founders of Children's Mercy:
Alice Berry Graham (left) and Katharine Berry Richardson.

Modern nursing's champion,
Florence Nightingale.

Father of American pediatrics,
Abraham Jacobi.

The playroom at Children's Mercy, 1920s.

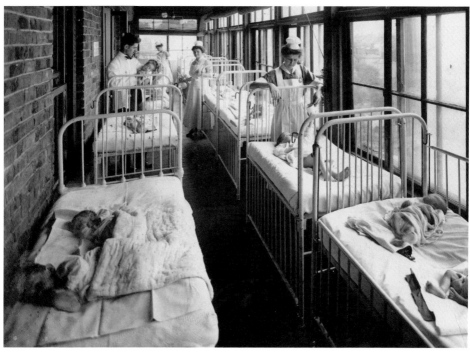

Ultraviolet rays at work: A sun porch at Children's Mercy.

An early exponent of psychosocial care, psychologist Erik Erikson.

Jean Piaget, who identified the phases children experience as they grow.

*Best-selling author and pediatrician
Benjamin Spock.*

Bettmann Archive

*He met children "where they're at":
T. Berry Brazelton.*

*Brazelton Touchpoints Center,
Boston Children's Hospital*

*Pediatrician — and mother — Penelope Leach:
"Only you really know your baby."*

Popperfoto/Getty Images

*Emma Plank, advocate for Child Life specialists
as part of the health team.*

CHAPTER 3

The transformation

As health care in the 1970s slowly embraced the growing movement of care, Children's Mercy stood as an early adopter.

Twenty years earlier, in the 1950s, the hospital with help from a grant had hired a full-time social worker to assist families and patients socially, financially and emotionally. In the mid-1960s, it had launched a program to address financial and accessibility needs of children in underserved areas of Kansas City.

Now, the campaign for a child-centered approach picked up momentum at Children's Mercy — although even there the commitment to and practice of psychosocial care remained far from universal.

Nursing leads the way

By and large, the care of children in the 1970s was provided by nurses. There was no "team approach" simply because there was no team. Many nurses worked 12-hour shifts. Before the hospital moved from its long-time home on Independence Avenue in 1970, many nurses lived in a dormitory next door. Nurses filled many roles for parents, who were still considered "visitors." Nurses told children stories. They rocked babies. They provided different means of comfort for psychological *and* medical needs.

"The child wasn't just a patient in a room," said Betty Boyd, a nurse who joined the hospital in 1964 and remained there until she retired 48 years later. "They were part of a family. I became part of their family, too."

At one point in her career, Boyd recalls, a survey team described Children's Mercy as a "we" hospital.

"It's always been that way," she said. "We get to know the patients, even in the emergency room. We'd work on a care plan that included specialty care, medication, home life."

Early in her career, nurses did a variety of jobs, work that today would be done by physical therapists, respiratory therapists and social workers. Nurses still sometimes perform those roles because they still spend the most time at a patient's bedside.

"We worked long shifts," Boyd said. "We listened to families. We worked *with* them."

Medical staff, busy concentrating on disease and injuries, was limited in both numbers and availability.

From the hospital's inception in the late 19th century until well into the 1970s, most of the physicians at Children's Mercy took no pay. Almost all were volunteers, with full-time outside practices.

It's not a stretch to say that nurses were the original medical social workers, as well as the original Child Life specialists.

Ramona Lindsey, another long-time nurse, came to Children's Mercy in 1965 while in nursing school in Fort Scott, Kansas.

"Physically, it was completely different than it is now," she said in 2017. "What hasn't changed is the fact that everyone still has the child's needs at heart. Everyone's focus is on what the child needs at the time and the parents need."

The influence of social work

The social influences on children's health had become apparent and unavoidable even before the 1970s. Among the programs begun in President Lyndon Johnson's Great Society and War on Poverty was the Children and Youth Project, undertaken at Children's Mercy and about 57 other hospitals across the country. The project aimed to increase access to health care for children living in poor inner-city neighborhoods. Under it, the hospital expanded its corps of social workers and other caregivers.

The advent of Medicare and Medicaid in 1965 opened the door to medical care for unprecedented numbers of children and adults. Children's Mercy, which was evolving from a purely charity hospital, needed to add programs, facilities and staff to meet the demand.

A big part of social workers' jobs in the 1970s involved child abuse. Child abuse was not new; one reason Children's Mercy was founded was to care for abused children. But in the 1970s children's rights began to be taken more seriously, and doctors and nurses became better at identifying abuse.

According to hospital documents, "in every suspected or identified case" of abuse, doctors admitted children to the hospital and contacted the social workers. The admission was not always for medical reasons, it was to protect the child. This was one example of attempts to address *social* issues that could affect *physical* health.

There was much more to social workers' jobs. In fact, much of what today is handled by Child Life specialists or financial consultants and other professionals was part of the job of early social workers. And, before social workers, many of those jobs — if they were done at all — were the responsibility of nurses.

Some nurses and doctors struggled to accept social workers. Some questioned focus and others thought they might get in the way. Gradually, social workers became seen as a valuable part of a caregiving team. Not only was there plenty of

Social workers address a variety of needs

A 1970s policy document prepared by the Children's Mercy Social Services department explained the roles of social workers.

Problems of personal and social adjustment are brought to the Social Workers, who help people face the problems and find solutions. Sometimes solutions are found through a change in attitude or behavior, sometimes through modification of the environment.

A social worker must understand the emotional and social needs of the person and the community resources which can be mobilized on his behalf.

Some major areas in which we are called upon to offer our services:

I. Psychosocial Evaluations
    a. Neglect or deprivation
    b. Battered child
    c. Emotional problems
        i.   Parent-child relations
        ii. Marital problems
        iii. Individual's emotional instability
    d. School adjustment
    e. Ability of family to provide structure and care for convalescing child
    f. To help differentiate whether emotional basis exists in physical complaints
    g. Treatment of any of the above

II. Financial
    a. Hospital bill
    b. Living expenses while at hospital or at home

    c. Helping families arrange for continuing medi-
cal care after discharge
    d. Unemployment
    e. Transportation to and from the hospital

III. Discharge planning
IV. Supportive treatment
    a. To help the family through illness of child, acute or otherwise
    b. To help families adjusting to handicapped child
    c. Terminal illness of child
    d. Liaison between hospital and community agency, schools, etc., in sharing information in order to make best possible plan for patients

V. Miscellaneous
    a. Helping parents find lodging while child is hospitalized
    b. Helping plan for care of other children while one child in family is a patient
    c. Reporting sexual assaults of children
    d. Information relating to obtaining a baby by adoption
    e. Suggesting sources in local communities for emotional treatment
    f. To explore possibilities of more suitable school placement.
    g. Resources for special therapy, day care or pre-school
    h. Transfer of child to another hospital
    i. Work with child and family in observing medical regimen such as special diet or shots
    j. Family wishing to take child from hospital too soon
    k. Preventing school drop outs.

More generally, social workers deal with social or emotional problems with care interfering with the adjustment of the individual or family. These problems may or may not be related to medical care or physical condition.

work to go around but also growing evidence that social factors affected physical health and medical results.

In the 1980s, money began to dry up for some programs — the federal government had abandoned the Children and Youth Project — and health care entered a sustained era of cost containment. There was impetus to discharge patients quickly to ensure full reimbursement for services. That shifted priorities for many social workers to discharge planning: making sure that children were ready, medically and socially, to be released and that families were prepared to continue care, if necessary, at home.

This resulted in parents taking on an even greater role in their child's care, a role that many relished, but that some took on only hesitantly.

Parents as partners

Accepting parents as part of the health care team also has been part of the evolution.

"It's impossible to separate the kids' lives from the parents' lives," said Dr. Denise Dowd, a Children's Mercy emergency medicine and injury prevention specialist. "Parents are bathing their children in their environment. We need a multidisciplinary approach."

When Children's Mercy opened its Parent Care Unit in 1975, it clearly signaled a commitment to bring parents into a partnership role with doctors and nursing in caring for their children. It was a giant step.

An article about the unit appeared in the *Journal of the American Medical Association's* publication, *Medical News*.

"The facility ... increases the hospital's ability to care for patients while reserving acute care beds for those more seriously ill," the report said. "The facility also encourages close parent-child relationships during a stressful period."

The new unit, and the level of involvement of parents, was only the beginning. Although the dedicated Parent Care Unit eventually would close because of space constraints, parents would continue to play an increasingly important role in their child's care. In the 1990s, all patient rooms would become private and almost all would have beds for parents, who could stay around the clock.

Karen Cox, PhD, RN, who joined the hospital in 1987 and who would go on to serve as executive vice president and chief operating officer, said the pendulum of parental involvement swung back and forth for many years.

"Many health care providers thought families got in the way and that their presence diminished the child's ability to heal," she said in 2016. "I can't believe people thought that way. It was silly."

When Dr. Cox was nurse manager in the cancer unit, she decided to get more parents involved. One of her first projects: asking parents to help decorate the patient floor where many children and families spent days and weeks during long treatments for cancer.

One of those parents was Debbie Kerr, whose daughter, Charlotte, had a rare form of pancreatic cancer. Despite the absence of a treatment protocol — or doctors at Children's Mercy who had even seen that particular sickness — Kerr said the psychosocial touches that were coming of age in the late '80s and '90s made all the difference in the world.

"I was able to be at every CT and MRI to read her books and keep her calm," said Kerr, who in 2012 became manager of the Children's Mercy gift shops. "It makes a huge, huge difference."

Kerr said the hours she spent at the hospital as the parent of a patient showed her that children needed comfort beyond what was available from doctors and nurses. She often rocked babies herself or helped calm older children who were frightened or in pain at night.

"They welcomed us, and they made us feel at home," Kerr said. "This was our home away from home. They looked after *everything*. I'd do anything for this hospital."

Family involvement and other psychosocial measures were adopted in cancer programs before many others, according to a review of research and interviews with Children's Mercy employees. Why? Because of the potentially disastrous consequences of the disease and the length of time often needed for treatment.

"Oncology was one of the early adopters of the true multidisciplinary team in medicine," said Dr. Alan Gamis, head of the Division of Oncology who joined Children's Mercy in the 1980s. "And we recognize, because of the devastating news that we deliver, many families early on need social workers more than they need the doctors (before treatment begins).

"In the war on a child's cancer, we need social workers to help deal with the battlefield damage."

Outside of Children's Mercy, much has been written about the psychosocial implications of cancer diagnosis and treatment. Scientific journals, such as *Pediatric Blood Cancer* and the *Journal of Clinical Oncology*, have reported extensively on "the science of psychological care."

"A principle goal of psychosocial care is to recognize and address the effects that cancer and its treatment have on the medical status and emotional well-being of patients, their family members and their professional caregivers," according to the *Journal of Clinical Oncology*. "In addition to improving emotional well-being and mental health, provision of psychosocial care has been shown to yield better

Life on the cancer ward

Whitney E. Kerr Jr. wrote the book Flashing Bugs *about his daughter Charlotte's battle with cancer. In it, he described experiences he, his wife, Debbie Kerr, and Charlotte had at Children's Mercy, beginning in 1993, when Charlotte was 4, and continuing until she went to college in 2007. Here is an excerpt.*

As disappointed as she would get, Charlotte and her fellow patients found ways to make the best of it. And, excited about the approach of Halloween, Charlotte and another patient, Eric, worked an entire afternoon and turned Charlotte's room at Four North into a haunted house, complete with ghosts, skeletons, creepy music and spider webs.

Charlotte and Eric hid in the darkened bathroom with a flashlight, ready to jump out and scare those brave enough to venture in. Little Eric had a tough situation on the home front. He was an inner-city kid who had to take a cab ride to the hospital for his chemo treatments. He was the same age as Charlotte.

It was difficult for Charlotte and Eric to truly hide, hooked up as they were to their rolling IV trees, which were visible and obvious to those who came to visit this scary place. Apparently, the nurses, staff other patients and parents stopped by all day long to visit Charlotte's haunted house. It was quite a sensation and it did wonders for her spirits. Charlotte just kept improving. It amazed us how she bounced back after each treatment. Although she was fighting a cold, she had a healthy appetite and lots of energy.

Debbie had a much better handle on children like Eric, who mostly spent time on Four North alone. Many nights, she comforted children whose parents were away, rocking them to sleep. She usually did it after Charlotte was down for the night, but sometimes she'd pull Charlotte along in the red wagon. One of her favorites was an 18-month-old girl whose parents were unable to be there. That child cried every night, but Debbie was able to get her asleep. If, at that moment, Raphael could have come back to life and painted the scene of Debbie, Charlotte and that little girl, he would have named it "Madonna of Mercy."

As of 2019, Charlotte, by then 30 years old, was living, cancer-free, in Dallas. She was engaged to be married and volunteered to provide respite to cancer patients at Dallas Children's Hospital.

management of common disease-related symptoms and adverse effects of treatment such as pain and fatigue."

Dr. Gamis said family involvement was essential:

"If the family is unable, physically or mentally, to be compliant with the treatment, it will fail. Most families will do anything, absolutely anything. But what if they don't have the means? What if they just *can't?* What are the obstacles?"

He listed some of the possible complications: other siblings, transportation, finances, other family illnesses, employment and medical leave options. Childhood illnesses affect the whole family. As such, the needs of the family need to be considered if the care and treatment are going to be effective.

"Our philosophy is that the most important part of the care team is the family itself," Dr. Gamis said. "I like to tell parents our job is to educate them and at the end of the first month, they'll be telling us what to do."

As health care has continued to evolve, more treatment is done on an outpatient basis at clinics and even in homes. That forces families to take on greater responsibility for complicated, technical care.

As with other illnesses, cancer families fall into two categories, Dr. Gamis said. One is the parents who, metaphorically, lace up their boots and prepare for battle. The others, much fewer in number, find themselves overwhelmed, fearful or lost in self-pity. For the latter group, it is incumbent upon the psychosocial team to ensure they have the resources they need — emotionally and otherwise — to provide the care their children need.

Dr. Cox, the chief operating office, said her work with Debbie Kerr and other families in cancer opened the door for greater partnerships with families throughout the medical center. By 2016, families would play a central role in the operation of the hospital through family advisory boards (including one for Spanish-speaking families, another for medically complex children and others), through Family-Centered Care Advocates on staff and through direct involvement in hospital committees and work groups.

One of the first parents hired to give voice to those caregivers was Cheryl Chadwick. Her son, Kyle, was 6 years old in 2000 when he was diagnosed with leukemia. During his three years of chemotherapy, Kyle would spend months in the hospital, have dozens of surgeries and be seen by 20 different specialists. Kyle made it. He graduated from the University of Kansas School of Nursing in 2016.

"The doctors are the experts on the disease," Chadwick said. "It takes our collaboration. Parents know our kids best."

Throughout the Children's Mercy medical center and clinics, parents have influenced improvements in quality, the design of facilities and many other aspects of hospital operations. They also continue to have a direct role in the medical and psychosocial care of their children.

And it all started with a discussion about what color of curtains to buy.

Toward comprehensive care

One of the things driving the evolution of Children's Mercy into a true regional pediatric medical center — instead of the charity hospital that it had been for its first 60-plus years — was the desire of Kansas City leaders to provide the best possible care for all children, regardless of diagnosis, where they lived or what their family's bank account held.

In the 1960s and '70s, the hospital added new services and new doctors as pediatric specialties began to emerge and expand. The new building on Hospital Hill was almost immediately too small, and additions and remodeling became a constant of life.

The Central Governing Board in 1982 developed a broad mission statement that called for Children's Mercy to be a comprehensive pediatric medical center where "patients and their families are treated with consideration and understanding in a patient-centered environment."

The mission statement fueled even more growth and more dedication toward providing the full range of hospital services to all children. As psychosocial care grew in acceptance, this meant Children's Mercy would need to adopt new policies and hire new professionals.

By this time, Child Life professionals across the country had split off from the Association for the Care of Children's Health and formed their own trade association, the Child Life Council. The council had its first national meeting in 1982.

Children's Mercy would not hire its first certified Child Life specialist until the early 1990s, but it did hire patient activity coordinators to help provide some basic psychosocial care, such as play therapy.

Meanwhile, the role of social work continued to evolve. By the late 1980s, social workers were being encouraged by their leaders to seek out community partnerships to address problems that lay well beyond the walls of Children's Mercy.

Heather Brungardt, one of those social workers, said the leadership at Children's Mercy was innovative and understood the challenges of positioning social work to take more responsibility in providing whole-child care. That included finding new ways to participate in health care teams, helping families that were struggling with new medical diagnoses and assisting them in finding services to meet day-to-day needs.

In 2016, Brungardt was named the first head of the Children's Mercy Division of Psychosocial Services, which consists of nearly 250 full-time employees.

The role of spirituality

Children's Mercy hired its first chaplain, Dane Sommer, in 1987. Even though a volunteer network of chaplains had existed at the hospital part-time for nearly a century, he recalled that many people were unsure of his role.

"When I got here, there was really a big question about what you are supposed to do with a chaplain," said Sommer, who would still be at the hospital in the 2010s as head of Spiritual Services. Early on, he recalled, he came face-to-face with a surgeon as the two passed going in and out of a patient room. "He looked at me and said, 'Just so you know, we do medicine here,' as a way of dismissing the importance of my work."

Sommer, and the hospital, persisted. Slowly the role of spirituality and the need for chaplains were embraced. Not surprisingly, he sees the evolution of chaplaincy philosophically, if not spiritually:

"It has not been easy, but it has been a journey of compassion and excitement. In the hospital we recognize there is suffering, and it is hard to watch suffering, especially when it is children. Especially when there is nothing *we* can do. When we have no control. Our faith traditions provide us with a structure that can give us control."

Explaining the role of chaplains in providing comprehensive care, Dr. Randall L. O'Donnell, who joined Children's Mercy as president and CEO in 1993, said some people were confused by differences between spirituality and religion. Children's Mercy has been non-sectarian from its founding, meaning it does not subscribe to any religion or sect.

"All people are spiritual," Dr. O'Donnell said. "Not everyone is religious. Our spirituality is that part of us that enables us to have an awareness of the meaning of life and death, so we are empowered to face the ultimate challenges we encounter in our lives."

In 2012, the Lisa Barth Chapel opened, providing space for many activities and expanded the definition of "spiritual care." The new chapel was an expansion of chapels that had existed at the hospital since at least the early 1900s. Stained glass windows given to Children's Mercy in 1905 and 1908 are mounted on the wall outside the Lisa Barth Chapel as a reminder of our spiritual heritage.

"We have a place where all people are welcome," Sommer said, "where people of faith, people with a religious tradition or people who would describe themselves as non-believers or non-religious can come together and have a place they can go and … kneel and pray or they can go sit in quiet or they can read a book, listen to music — a gathering place."

....

CHAPTER 4

A spark

As the 1990s began, Children's Mercy — with a newly declared mission to be the region's comprehensive pediatric medical center — was poised for bigger and better things.

Its financial fortunes were turning around. It had new plans for fundraising, growth and expansion. There was momentum and there were big dreams. But it was also emerging from some exhausting battles over physical expansion.

The hospital had a strategic plan. Yet its leadership often wound up reacting, not leading, said Mary Jane Barnes, chair of the hospital's Central Governing Board in 1991-92 and a member of the CEO search committee.

The Board, also recognizing increased competition for parts of the pediatric business and increased pressure to control costs, sought a leader who could provide stability, encourage growth and help the hospital reach beyond its traditional self. It wanted someone who could help complete the transformation of Children's Mercy to the hospital where children and their families wanted to be, instead of where they had to be.

In 1993, the board found what it was looking for, hiring Randall L. O'Donnell, PhD, as president and chief executive officer.

"We needed someone who could *develop* the vision for the hospital, lead us to it," Barnes said. "I could tell, the first time I spent the morning with him, that he had a vision. He could walk it, he talked it and he could do it. That is what we needed."

Just what was the hospital getting in Dr. O'Donnell? The story began decades before he arrived in Kansas City.

"We always need to be getting better"

Growing up in the Pacific Northwest, Rand O'Donnell was introduced to children's health care by his mother, a pediatric nurse. As he learned about some of the joys and challenges of taking care of children, the seeds of compassion and the desire to help were planted. His dad was a high school teacher and coach, further sowing a wish to serve children and young people.

Recalling those early days, Dr. O'Donnell remembers the battles his mother waged with medical staff and administrators to allow parents to spend the night in the hospital with their children. In Indiana and the rest of the United States in the 1960s, such things were unheard of. Doctors and others noted that children became emotional and disruptive around the times parents visited. Parents, they reasoned, must be part of the problem.

But Mrs. O'Donnell knew intuitively — and scientific studies supported her belief — that the acting up arose from separation anxiety and the stress of hospitalization. It happened not because their parents were visiting, but because the children had to stay in the hospital after the parents departed.

Teenaged Rand O'Donnell listened to his mom tell those stories, and he was drawn to opportunities to comfort children and improve their hospital experience. He became a surgery orderly at his mom's hospital, where he had more experiences that fueled his passion.

On one occasion, O'Donnell saw firsthand how a frightened child needed to be comforted, not shamed. One young patient was fearful and lonely because her parents were not nearby. Another orderly yelled at her, said she was bothering other patients and told her to be quiet. His rudeness and uncaring attitude had just the opposite effect. Her crying intensified and O'Donnell's job of keeping her calm became impossible.

After she was safely in the operating room, O'Donnell followed that orderly to the locker room and did something he had never done before or since: he shoved him up against the wall and told him to back off.

"Don't you get it?" he asked. "They need our help. We're here to take care of them, not yell at them."

That was how he discovered a special sensitivity to the emotional needs of children.

Another time, he was assigned to escort a patient to an ear, nose and throat exam. As he began to wheel her down the hall, he offhandedly told her it was just a short trip.

"But when I told her I was taking her to the operating room, she fell apart," he recalled during a talk in 2004. "She thought she was just coming in and someone would look at her throat, which is what we were doing. But they did that in the OR and she just lost it. She was scared something was really wrong with her and nobody told her.

"I felt terrible about it and it took the nurses and doctors in the operating room half an hour to calm her down before they could do the test.

"That's when I began to understand the importance of communication with patients, the need to be careful with the words we use and the need to prepare them for what's going to happen."

Another lesson came one night when a woman went into premature labor and delivered a tiny baby. The mom got to see her little girl and give her a kiss, and then a nurse took her away. Later, Dr. O'Donnell learned the baby would not survive. At the time, there was simply no way to save such a fragile infant.

"I didn't comprehend that we couldn't save premature infants," he said. "That's when babies just died. There was nothing we could do.

"And I think that was the seed of my notion that we always need to do new things. We always need to be getting better. We have to invest in research so moms don't have to go through what that mom did, and so we can save those little babies and they can go on and thrive like they do today."

A bit later, while he pursued his undergraduate degree in economics at California Lutheran College in Thousand Oaks, California, Dr. O'Donnell and one of his brothers worked as orderlies at a hospital. As he recalls, someone brought in a tricycle to entertain the children. His brother helped one little leukemia patient zoom up and down the halls, a big smile on his face, the breeze rushing over the child's bald head, wafting his cares away. One of the nurses questioned whether that was appropriate in a hospital, but O'Donnell's brother persisted, delighting the children — and harming none, Dr. O'Donnell pointed out.

Recalling another instance, when he and others pushed patients on gurneys in a mock race, Dr. O'Donnell jokingly suggested a research study to demonstrate how the excitement increased heart and breathing rates and improved blood oxygen saturation!

It was also in California that Dr. O'Donnell's approach to management took root. Working nights in an orthopedic unit, he was struck by the way staff morale and unit operations were affected by different management styles:

"We could have a full staff of nurses and orderlies and if there was a certain nurse in charge, it was chaos. Her attitude was always 'the sky is falling.' And yet, when there was another nurse in charge, even if it was just her and me and a full unit of patients, things went smoothly. She was calm and showed confidence and we got the jobs done."

While working on his PhD in hospital and health administration at the University of Iowa in the mid-1970s, O'Donnell dug deeper into the effects of hospitalization on children. Few professors were enthusiastic about his work, suggesting he was limiting himself by focusing on pediatrics.

But his review of previous research showed a solid foundation for expanding psychosocial practices, such as parental visitation. While he interned as part of his PhD program in hospital management at the Crippled Children's Hospital in Richmond, Virginia, O'Donnell conducted his own research into how hospitalization changed children's behavior. He found evidence that supported increased visits by parents, and that showed the need to understand outside influences, such as parents' economic status, in considering children's emotional response.

His dissertation, "The Psychological Effects of Childhood Hospitalization: Implications for Pediatric Health Care Delivery," was designed to provide a scientific call to action for increased application of psychosocial practices. It concluded by urging more research and the development of profiles showing which patients might be susceptible to psychological harm. That eventually led to the creation of psychosocial screening tools that today are routinely used at hospitals around the country.

Armed with his postgraduate degree in 1977, the newly minted Dr. O'Donnell moved to New York. There he put his passion for psychosocial care to work as an associate administrator at the Children's Hospital of Buffalo.

At the time, the hospital had one half-time "play lady" who helped with the emotional care of children. Dr. O'Donnell worked to expand that role and created the hospital's first Child Life program. He developed policies, procedures and checklists to guide a new psychosocial program. His commitment there was acknowledged in one of the seminal textbooks on the subject: *Child Life in Hospitals: Theory and Practice*, by Richard H. Thompson and Gene Stanford, published in 1981 and still in circulation.

From there, he moved to Arkansas Children's Hospital in Little Rock, where he was chief operating officer and then chief executive officer from 1980 to 1993. When he arrived, Dr. O'Donnell recalled, the hospital was basically an orphanage for poor, sick children. As in Buffalo, the hospital had a half-time "play lady," but little else to engage the children's emotional and social needs. So in addition to expanding the clinical programs — enabling the hospital to care for more children — Dr. O'Donnell hired a Child Life specialist from a hospital in Florida and told her to build a program.

"She got herself battered and bruised (in spirit) in a hospital that had never heard of Child Life," Dr. O'Donnell said. "And she stuck with it. I give her an awful lot of credit."

A defining moment at Arkansas Children's occurred at a medical staff meeting when a nephrologist challenged Dr. O'Donnell about what the doctors considered a waste of money.

"A Child Life person has never saved a child's life," the nephrologist said.

Before Dr. O'Donnell could respond, another doctor, a well-regarded orthopedist, cleared his throat. "That may be," he said, "but at least the kids don't have to lie in cribs all day staring at the ceiling."

Dr. O'Donnell smiled at the memory:

"That was the end of that discussion about wasting money on Child Life."

"Nurturing Leadership" faces challenges

For the health care industry, much of the last 50 years has been marked by concerns about expenses. Advances in medicine have brought new techniques, new pharmaceuticals and new machines — and all have come at a cost. Financial matters and discussions of "cost containment" are a part of every leader's agenda. For children's hospitals, the pressures have been equally strong, and perhaps more so because of the high percentage of patients with Medicaid or without any medical insurance at all.

When many administrators seek to cut or contain costs, they look at areas that don't generate revenue, areas such as Child Life and Social Work.

"All too often," Dr. O'Donnell wrote in 1987, "budget limitations are used as the excuse for neglect of psychosocial programs. If there is commitment by the hospital leadership and if the hospital staff is willing to be creative and resourceful, children and families can be assured of the psychosocial services that are such an important part of their total care."

That kind of care, he said, did not have to cost a lot of money.

Writing in the *Journal of the Association for the Care of Children's Health* when he was CEO of Arkansas Children's, Dr. O'Donnell said that psychosocial care was "not a frill, something that can be easily eliminated or scaled down when the financial going gets tough."

"Instead," he wrote, even in an era of cost containment it was "a basic component of the process of caring for children ... both imperative and achievable."

Despite financial pressures at Arkansas Children's — where 40 percent of patients were on Medicaid and 20 percent more had no third-party coverage — the hospital under Dr. O'Donnell managed to build and sustain a psychosocial program that was recognized for its quality in 1985 by the Association for the Care of Children's Health. He developed a four-part strategy for taking care of the whole child, a strategy he would take to Children's Mercy eight years later:

1. Begin with a commitment at the highest levels. Make it a priority.
2. Make all employees, not just specialized professionals, responsible for psychosocial care.

3. Adopt hospital policies and practices that enhance psychosocial care.

4. Turn to outside sources for special projects.

It was also in his time in Arkansas that his distinctive leadership style emerged.

In 1992, Dr. O'Donnell wrote *Nurturing Leadership*, a small book that detailed his management philosophy. It provided a blueprint for how he would operate Children's Mercy. Although designed for business leaders in any industry, the book drew on his pediatric hospital experience and demonstrated his method of caring for all of a child's needs.

"At new employee orientation, I review [our hospital credo] and explain that the most important aspect of any job within our organization is the emotional support of our children and their families," Dr. O'Donnell wrote. With that, he set the tone that everyone's job — not just the job of social workers or of chaplains or of Child Life specialists, but of everyone — was psychosocial care.

Part of his management philosophy, he wrote, was hiring the right people and getting out of their way. When employees felt good about themselves, he said, they could feel good about their employer and do their best work.

"I inform each new employee of our hospital that he or she is the key to our excellence," he wrote in *Nurturing Leadership*. "Bulldoze the buildings, scrap the equipment and pitch a huge tent, I say, and as long as we still have you, we will still have the best children's hospital in the world."

Some employees — especially those without day-to-day contact with children and their families — might not believe that psychosocial needs were part of their jobs. Disagreeing, Dr. O'Donnell offered a story from Little Rock:

"A 9-year-old patient was in his room, alone, watching television one morning. A young maintenance worker carrying a plumber's snake walked into the room and headed to the bathroom to work on a stopped-up commode. He didn't say anything, just walked right in and went to work. The young boy went screaming out of the room, crying down the hallway.

"It turns out that the little boy thought the plumber's snake was meant to go down his throat, not the commode. Why did he think this? Well, everyone else who had come into his room for the last week and half had been there to poke, prod, test and examine him.

"This story illustrates just how much we believe in honesty and communication with our families. These elements are essential to meeting the goals of emotional support."

Nurturing Leadership emphasizes that hands-on, personalized psychosocial care goes hand-in-hand with the finest medical care.

Lighting the fire in Kansas City

In the early 1990s, Dr. O'Donnell was not seeking to leave Little Rock. Yet when his name came up in the search for a new CEO in Kansas City, he decided to take a look. For one thing, it was closer to his wife's family in Iowa. For another, there were big dreams at Children's Mercy in Kansas City, and he loved a challenge. Besides, he had some big ideas of his own.

Children's Mercy was emerging from a long and raucous civic battle over the preservation of decades-old buildings that once housed Kansas City's old General Hospital. The buildings stood in the way of Children's Mercy expansion on Hospital Hill. The hospital also was in the midst of a fundraising campaign to update its facilities and programs. It had begun to open medical clinics outside the central city to improve access for suburban families.

When he moved to Kansas City, Dr. O'Donnell set out, with the help of a supportive board of directors and others in the community, to finish the transformation of Children's Mercy from a successful charity hospital into a leading pediatric academic medical center. The Board wanted to see the physical expansion of the hospital completed, but also envisioned expanding the medical staff and offering more programs so the children of Kansas City would have everything they needed in their hometown children's hospital.

During the job negotiations, Dr. O'Donnell explained his commitment to psychosocial care and its importance in the care for children. He asked for a strong commitment in Kansas City. And he got it.

Early in his tenure at Children's Mercy — which would last more than 25 years — he stunned some on the staff by declaring that his goal was to make Kansas City's children's hospital the best in the world.

"The first time I heard him speak, I thought he was crazy," recalled a smiling Dr. Cox. "He said we were going to be the best children's hospital in the world, and I thought somebody in the interview process didn't give him the whole scoop.

"But after I saw some of the things he did, I began to believe."

Change was coming. As Marvin Kolb, MD, the medical director at Children's Mercy when Dr. O'Donnell arrived, put it: "Hold on!"

The best in the world

What Dr. O'Donnell did first was to articulate what Jim Collins, the author of the business text *Good to Great*, called the BHAG — Big, Hairy, Audacious Goal. Set the bar high.

Dr. O'Donnell did: "We will be the best in the world."

Next, he told employees there was one guiding principle: every decision, from the small to the significant, should be based on the best interests of patients and families.

Then he told them to get to work! He was open to change. He and other leaders knew that not every new idea or approach would be successful. But they would keep trying.

Dr. O'Donnell knew the transformation faced challenges.

As he had seen in Arkansas, the medical staff was reluctant to embrace the introduction of Child Life specialists, more social workers and full-time chaplains. Doctors, because of their advanced medical knowledge and unique skills, often considered themselves independent and shunned help that was not directly related to their specialty. As years went by, Dr. O'Donnell saw many of them drop their objections and welcome psychosocial help.

When Children's Mercy introduced mandatory interpersonal training for all staff in the middle 1990s called "First Impressions" and "Great Explanations," there was pushback.

At one meeting of the medical staff, Dr. O'Donnell sat nervously as the chief of surgery rose to tell his colleagues about his experience.

"I had my reservations," the esteemed doctor said. "I've been practicing for 40 years. But I went to that and I learned a lot. And some of you out there really need it!"

In the expansion of psychosocial programs, Dr. O'Donnell credits the "heroes" he works with for being the boots on the ground.

Just months after he arrived at Children's Mercy, Dr. O'Donnell hired Stacey Koenig as the first director of Child Life programming. Koenig was familiar with Dr. O'Donnell, having worked at Arkansas Children's. Her family had recently moved to Kansas City.

Children's Mercy had long recognized the importance of letting kids be kids, and had a Patient Activities Department to engage children and distract them from the disruptions caused by hospitalization. Donations of toys and games helped keep the children busy. What was lacking was a strategy and the professional grounding of certified Child Life specialists.

Child Life, at the basic level, works to make things comfortable for patients and families by helping reduce stress and cope with their emotions and by encouraging them to learn and grow during their stay.

From early in the inception of the Child Life program, specialists scheduled play sessions. But instead of play for its own sake, this was play that had medical context. The goal was to find a healthy way for children to "embrace" what was going on around them. Child Life specialists helped children learn to cope, to swallow pills and to follow doctors' orders.

The specialists brought out syringes, bandages and other things children often experienced in the hospital. During play, the children could express their anxieties and their fears. Unknown and misunderstood things became known and understood, and the children's anxiety dropped.

A watershed moment occurred in the middle 1990s with Dr. Stanley Hellerstein, a kidney specialist who had been on the staff since the 1960s.

"Dr. Hellerstein was working on a procedure where the children had to give a urine sample and they would just freeze," Koenig recalled. "They couldn't get the kids to do it because they were scared. They felt such a loss of control."

Child Life specialists went to work, helping the patients understand that they had a job to do, and that there would be a beginning and an end to the process. That helped the children emotionally and helped the doctors and other staff get their jobs done.

Dr. Hellerstein reported the success to the medical staff. Doing procedures without Child Life present, he said, was not doing right by the child or the test itself. Coming from a respected member of the medical staff, the comments further validated Child Life.

Child Life has grown to include many kinds of therapy, some involving music and even dogs.

In the late '90s, the Child Life team members persuaded the Radiology staff to allow them to test a theory: that helping prepare children for MRIs and CT scans and staying with them during the procedures would increase efficiency, satisfaction and safety.

Before the procedures, Child Life staffers showed children photos and wooden models of the equipment and played recordings of sounds the machines made. They eased fears by explaining the process using sensitive, age-appropriate language. The Child Life specialists then accompanied patients into the examination room and stayed there to comfort or distract them with bubbles or music or movies. The pilot project was a huge success.

In 1998, before the trial began, 16 percent of children needed to be sedated for an MRI so they would lie still. Sedation increased the time of the MRI process, increased the cost and added to the risk simply because sedation is not 100 percent safe.

By 2003, the rate of sedation had dropped below 5 percent, despite a 40 percent increase in cases. The average scan time was reduced from 90 minutes to 15.

Kids are the bosses

Although Children's Mercy has a long history of putting children first, Dr. O'Donnell has a unique take on that. He likes to refer to children as "the bosses." He had special business cards printed and handed them out to children he met. Not his business cards, theirs. The cards have a place for their names and the title underneath says, "The Boss."

What does that mean, exactly?

In Dr. O'Donnell's mind, and the minds of the devotees to the philosophy, it means that in *every case*, hospital staff must listen to children (and their parents) and try to provide for their wants and needs. Pizza for breakfast? Check! A formal prom dance for teens unable to leave the hospital? Check! Day passes for patients who are suffering "cabin fever?" Check!

He used this illustration in his *Nurturing Leadership* book from an episode at Arkansas Children's:

"A visitor to our hospital once caught the full sense of its culture after she became irritated at a young patient who nearly brushed her with his tricycle as he rode down the hallway.

"'Why do they let him do that?' she complained to her companion. One of our nurses overheard the impatient remark and retorted, 'Because it is *his* hospital.'"

Sometimes, the "kids are the bosses" runs up against policies and procedures that are ingrained in the staff. Still, Dr. O'Donnell says, it's the needs of the children and their parents that should be protected, not a we've-always-done-it-this-way mentality.

"No policy should be so entrenched that simple exceptions cannot be made," he said. "Enabling employees and managers to exercise their own good judgment for the benefit of one another and their customers is helpful to all concerned. Here again, the enabling tone needs to be set on Day One of employment. I tell orientees that the only ways to get into trouble are by being rude to a child or parent or by breaking the law."

For children to truly be the bosses, they need a voice. Sometimes, the patients are too young or too scared to speak up. Their parents are their advocates and the staff of the children's hospital needs to listen to them.

Easier said than done.

Ginny Miller's first visits to Children's Mercy did not give her the most favorable impression. In the mid-1980s, she was new to Kansas City. She had two young sons and a daughter, Lisa, a quadriplegic with cerebral palsy who was born in 1986. Shortly after her birth, Lisa became a patient at Children's Mercy. What her mom found was a hospital where children may well have been its first and only priority, but where family-centered care was still a budding concept and hospital operations were designed around doctors and the rest of the staff.

"There was a lot of compassion, but there was not a lot of support," she recalled. "I would see families in the waiting rooms and you could tell they had given up."

At the time, Children's Mercy was widely considered a hospital of "last resort," where patient and families went because they had no choice, either because of finances or because there was no other place in town with as much pediatric expertise. In the late 1980s and early 1990s, the hospital's physical environment was somewhat drab and beaten up. Uncomfortable chairs filled waiting rooms and lined the hallways. Sometimes things weren't clean

Ginny Miller complained. She offered suggestions. Little changed. Altering a culture is an arduous job. In addition, hospital finances were tight; the budget was unbalanced. Many parents grew to accept less-than-optimum service and surroundings.

Over time, Miller grew frustrated with long waits, with doctors missing appointments, with a lack of communication, with the nightmare of scheduling visits to multiple clinics, with a general lack of respect or understanding for families and particularly with one nurse. That nurse, trying to protect a doctor from Miller's anger, told her the clinic visit was cancelled because Miller was too frustrated to see the doctor.

Physical surroundings began to change slowly in the mid-1990s. The budget improved with new tax support and as new insurance contracts began to attract more patients. New buildings opened, offering more space for operations, a brighter environment and an opportunity to remodel older parts of the hospital.

The patient-first, family-centered mentality was taking root among staff, but it did not become widespread overnight.

On a particularly bad day in the late 1990s, Miller called Linda Taloney, who was Patient Advocate.

"I finally said, 'This must change,'" she recalled in 2018, remembering the frustration of trying to juggle her daughter's care and a son's need for surgery. "With Linda, I found understanding. She talked me off the cliff."

Taloney was new to a job, created in 1998, that was evolving to provide a larger voice for parents. The day Miller called was another step in that process. Miller, outspoken and frustrated, had found a sounding board.

Both Taloney and Dr. Cox, the COO, wanted to expand the role of parents. Miller was invited in 1998 to join the Patient Care and Family Environment Committee, along with three other parents. Initially, the parents' role was limited to listening to staff reports. But they wanted to actively participate. The committee morphed into the Family Advisory Board in 2003.

"Our goal was not to be hospital-bashing," Miller said. "But they needed the parent voice. It was important for me to get over my pain and do something positive."

Once, a dispute arose over parking spaces for vehicles designed for people in wheelchairs. Hospital staff cited industry standards and declared that there were plenty of handicapped-accessible spots. Miller argued that the standards were inadequate. She escorted the director of facilities to the parking garage to demonstrate the difficulty of getting a wheelchair out of her van in the designated spaces. Hospital leadership decided to increase the size of handicapped parking spaces.

Miller was hired on staff in 2006, a landmark decision in the role of parents. She left the hospital when Lisa graduated from high school in 2008 and she needed time to take care of her daughter. But Ginny Miller's impact has been lasting.

Looking at the hospital through the eyes of the parents is what led to the 1996 opening of the first Ronald McDonald House Family Room anywhere inside a children's hospital.

"We saw parents sleeping on the floor next to their children," said Brad Warady, MD, head of the department of Nephrology and a strong advocate of family-centered care. "That's not helping them. If parents are tired, they can't help their kids.

"They don't want to be here, but they want to be with their kids. We needed to find a way to make that happen."

Working with Ronald McDonald House Charities, Children's Mercy found some room just down the hall from the Pediatric Intensive Care Unit to build a quiet space with a living room, kitchen and several small bedrooms for people to spend the night. Now, parents no longer must leave the building for the Ronald McDonald House down the street or their homes to get a break.

In addition, as their children's primary support, parents should understand how to talk with their children about medical conditions and procedures.

"When we work with the kids, parents are on the edge of their seats," Koenig said. "We want to teach them, too. We are treating the family, not just the kids. That's really important."

As a teen volunteer at his mom's hospital, Dr. O'Donnell had seen the effects of stress on children. As a hospital leader, he knew it was his responsibility to do all he could to promote the well-being of children and their families.

"By helping create a child-friendly atmosphere," he said, the efforts of Child Life staff "are essential to healing."

He puts chaplaincy and social work — two other roles dedicated solely to psychosocial care — on the same plane.

"Our spirituality becomes particularly engaged when we face illness or injury, suffering or death," he said. "Our chaplains develop relationships with each patient and family. They offer encouragement and comfort — on good days and not-so-good days — and help families make decisions at a time when none of their options are the ones they want."

Social workers, likewise, work with families struggling to accept and cope with new life challenges. The surge of life's complications outside the hospital walls has increased pressures. Social workers' responsibilities have changed and grown. They find themselves looking even more to outside groups and organizations that partner with families for food, clothing, housing, transportation, legal help and more.

All three of these roles — Child Life, chaplaincy and social work — have met with doubts from some medical professionals. However, with the support of Dr. O'Donnell and other key leaders such as the chiefs of nursing and operations and financial officers with administrative oversight, their work and their care has become sewn into the fabric of Children's Mercy.

By the late 1990s, as reluctant staff saw the impact of all these efforts, it became easier to accept them as an important part of comprehensive, best-practices care.

Outsiders notice the change

In 2005, the Robert Wood Johnson Foundation asked Children's Mercy to chronicle its decade-long cultural transformation, its success in going from "good to great." It was one of only 10 hospitals in the United States chosen to document its effort, and the only children's hospital in the group. Children's Mercy was singled out as a model for improving culture to more effectively meet the needs of patients, to promote a positive work environment and to support the goals of the organization.

Over the course of a year, project managers interviewed dozens of hospital employees and community members and looked at data from a variety of sources. The result was a booklet, "Listening, Leading, Learning," which outlined six steps Children's Mercy had taken from 1995 to 2006. Five of the steps were articulating a bold vision, viewing all employees as essential contributors, expecting and encouraging excellence, staying open to failure and responsive to change and repositioning the organization externally.

The sixth step, of particular importance here, was: "Place patients and families first." Within that step, there were three key components:

- Make patient impact the focus of all decisions.
- Acknowledge and address the psychosocial needs of patients and families

- Meaningfully involve patients and families in decision-making throughout the organization.

Armed with data that showed results — among them higher patient satisfaction scores — the report for Robert Wood Johnson suggested that the patient-first, psychosocial model was working.

"The results of this work are more than 'feel good,'" the report states. "In fact, the [Child Life] department's significant success in reducing sedation rates among those needing CT Scans is an example worthy of case study in medical journals."

As the Robert Wood Johnson Foundation had discovered, it was hard to ignore Children's Mercy's success on a variety of fronts. The impact of psychosocial care was undeniable, and it was spreading. As its acceptance and implementation evolved and grew, children and their families reaped the rewards.

Transformation is not quick or easy. But with skilled and understanding leadership and dedicated and innovative staff, Children's Mercy found itself on a course toward providing the best possible care for the *whole* child and his or her family.

Dr. O'Donnell and the other early advocates of psychosocial and family-centered care knew success depended on a team effort. Everyone had to embrace and enhance psychosocial care.

It was not a one-size-fits-all approach. Yet, following Dr. O'Donnell's philosophy of commitment at the highest levels, hiring the right people, putting patients and families first and providing a nurturing environment, Children's Mercy not only survived the journey of transformation, it thrived.

And so, too, for the most part, have the children and families in its care.

CHAPTER 5

The embrace of family-centered care

When the Institute of Medicine issued its report, "To Err is Human," in 1999, it shook the health care industry.

Many studies from the nonprofit, independent agency, which is part of the National Academy of Sciences, are put on shelves and forgotten. But this one painted a devasting picture of health care in the United States, and it could not be ignored.

With its follow-up report two years later, "Crossing the Quality Chasm," the institute outlined problems nationwide with quality, efficiency, effectiveness, timeliness and patient-centeredness. The problems went far beyond disappointing. Too often, they proved fatal.

By neglecting those problems, the reports found, health care was failing. Through preventable errors, it was killing as many as 98,000 people a year.

The Institute of Medicine, renamed the National Academy of Medicine in 2015, was founded in 1970 by Congress to provide unbiased advice to the country on medicine, biomedicine and health. Its parent organization, the National Academy of Sciences, dated back to 1863.

"The IOM report woke everyone up," said Dr. Cox, chief operating officer for Children's Mercy until 2018.

Too many hospitals, she said, thought, "Yes, there are some things that happen, but they just happen.

"That was the attitude."

With American hospitals' dirty laundry aired in public, that attitude needed to change if hospitals, doctors and the entire industry were to maintain public trust.

Decades in coming

Part of the failing was that hospitals were ignoring patient's needs and rights.

The two studies by the Institute of Medicine gave new credence to patient- and family-centered care. That kind of care was more than sentimental; it was essential to higher quality and better results.

Just as the concept and practice of psychosocial care developed gradually, so did the idea of patient- and family-centered care. Family-centered care had its roots in the consumer and family-support movements that began in the 1960s.

In his State of the Union address to Congress in 1962, President John Kennedy outlined rights of consumers of health care and other human services: to be safe and informed, to choose, and to be heard. In that speech, much of Kennedy's focus was on creating national health insurance for seniors (what would become Medicare), but he also mentioned the importance of providing care for families, vaccinations for children and protection from habit-forming drugs and unsafe practices.

Beverly Johnson, who helped found the Association for the Care of Children's Health in the mid-1960s before starting the Institute for Patient- and Family-Centered Care, said changing demographics — including both parents working outside the home — created a need for increased support for families.

Advances in technology, medical science and specialization led to improvements in patient care. Yet some of those improvements came at the expense of creating a distance between children and their doctors and nurses.

"We must keep health care human," Dr. O'Donnell said in a presentation at Milwaukee Children's Hospital in 2004. "Technology seems to always push us in the opposite direction."

Even though the concept of patient-centeredness was not new by the turn of the 21st century, much of it was still dismissed by many in health care as trivial, superficial and unrealistic.

Critics, according to a variety of journal articles from the time, suggested that doctors knew best and did not need parents' or patients' help. Patients, the argument went, would be driven by their egos or sympathies, not by evidence. Following their whims would be disruptive, inefficient and ineffective. The critics asked, Where's the science?

Proponents were patient and persisted.

By 2011, an article in the *Annals of Family Medicine* concluded: "There have been concerns that patient-centered care, with its focus on individual needs, might be at odds with an evidence-based approach, [but] ... a good outcome must be defined in terms of what is meaningful and valuable to the individual patient."

The Association for the Care of Children's Health became an early champion of family-centered care, saying that parents and other family members had a profound influence on the health of children. In the 1980s, the association worked with Dr. C. Everett Koop, surgeon general of the United States, to address the needs of families of special-needs children. ACCH itself was learning the importance of involving parents.

Although from the start the association had representatives from a variety of health care disciplines, Johnson pointed out in a 2018 interview that at first families were not involved.

"We soon learned that was a mistake," she said.

In a 2000 article on the history of the family-centered care movement, Johnson said:

"Not only is the family the primary unit for the delivery of health services to infants and children, but the family environment is probably the greatest influence on a child's health. ... Our growing recognition of the psychological and social components of health has enhanced awareness of the family's importance. ... Health care providers can support, encourage and enhance the competence of parents in their role as caregivers."

One of the world's leading advocates of patient-centered care (which it has renamed "person-centered") has been The Picker Institute, founded in 1986. During Jean Picker's treatment for a terminal condition, institute founders Jean and Harvey Picker saw an American health care system that was technologically and scientifically outstanding. But they believed it was not adequately sensitive to the concerns and personal needs of patients. That lack of sensitivity affected the quality of care they received.

On behalf of the Picker Institute and The Commonwealth Fund, researchers from Harvard Medical School in 1987 defined eight principles of patient-centered care:

- Respect for patients' values, preferences and expressed needs
- Coordination and integration of care
- Information, communication and education
- Physical comfort
- Emotional support and alleviation of fear and anxiety
- Involvement of family and friends
- Continuity and transition
- Access to care

Throughout his career, Dr. O'Donnell has emphasized that everyone's job is patient care. At orientation for new employees at Children's Mercy, instruction is given on the concepts of patient- and family-centered and psychosocial care. Staff with direct patient care — nurses for instance — take part in an expanded orientation program that includes conversations with Child Life, Social Work, Chaplaincy and other professionals. They tell new nurses that they can't do it alone; it takes everyone at Children's Mercy to care for the needs of the children and their families.

The Picker Institute's Family-Centered Care Improvement Guide, produced in 2008, agrees:

"Perhaps the greatest influences on the patient experiences are the individuals who comprise the hospital staff. Whether at the bedside or in the back office, in a patient-centered hospital, every staff member contributes to the overall patient experience. From ensuring linens are fresh and bathrooms are clean to following up on billing questions and compiling customized patient information packets, every interaction is an opportunity for caring, support and compassion.

"Patient input confirms that it is often the simple acts of caring that are most meaningful; conversely, the absence of caring attitudes and caring gestures can leave a lasting impression."

A *Harvard Business Review* article in May 2017 by Thomas H. Lee, MD, explained the power of engaging all employees in providing family-centered and psychosocial care:

"If they believe the organization cares about quality and safety and if the core values include compassion for patients and teamwork, there is a good chance that better quality and financial performance will follow."

A report in the *Family Health Care Journal* by Beverly Johnson echoed those comments: "Studies documented the cost effectiveness of family-centered approaches in terms of reduced emergency department visits and fewer readmissions to the hospital."

With scientific studies showing better patient outcomes and a better bottom line, it was becoming easier to persuade hospital staff to change the way they did business. But for family-centered and psychosocial care to be truly effective, the right kind of people had to be in place.

Hiring well

Dr. Cox, the former chief operating officer, remembered interviewing a candidate for a nursing job when she was nurse manager in the cancer unit. She asked the candidate why she wanted to work at Children's Mercy.

"She told me she didn't like working with adults, so she wanted to work with kids," Dr. Cox said. "I told her she was in the wrong place."

How's that? For sure, there are kids to be taken care of at Children's Mercy. But there are plenty of adults in the picture, too. When it comes to parents or grandparents, they may be more actively involved in their child's care than in their own.

Don't want to work with grown-ups? Don't come to work here, was the message.

Plenty of people do want to work at Children's Mercy. In 2017, more than 30,000 job applications were filed. That averaged more than 80 people a day, every day of the year, seeking one of the about 8,000 jobs at the hospital. Some jobs, particularly those at entry level, attracted hundreds of applications. For other, more specialized, jobs there were fewer, and in some cases incentives were offered to attract candidates. Of the 30,000 applications, Children's Mercy filled 1,899 positions.

Recruiters in Human Resources work hard to make sure they place the right people in the right jobs. It takes balance. There are many different jobs at Children's Mercy and many different personalities, education levels and skills needed to fill them. But Molly Weaver, the director of talent acquisition, and the other recruiters said all employees had one thing in common: they understand what it means to put kids first.

"I can hear it in their voices," said Julie Aust, a recruiter who says in her online profile that, as much as she likes working at Children's Mercy, her most important job is that of being a mom to two children. "They understand what it means when we say, 'Kids are the bosses.' Their faces light up. They are just so excited to be here."

Many of the people who apply for jobs are parents whose own child has been cared for at Children's Mercy. They've seen the care from the other side of the bed, and they believe Children's Mercy is where they want to be.

"If their experience tells them this is where they want to be, that's an advantage," said Angie Richardson, Talent Acquisition Manager. She and others said the willingness to help others the way they had been helped was a powerful motivator.

"There has to be a commitment to the kids," said recruiter Jeff Janda. "If not, they won't last for long. This is not Disneyland. There are sick children here. Do they love children when they're sick? Are they here for the right reasons?"

Job candidates can choose a video job application that features children asking the questions. Other candidates will get an opportunity to shadow employees in the jobs they are interested in. It's all about ensuring the right fit.

"We want you to self-select out if this isn't for you," Weaver said. "We are looking for special people. We are looking for people who will do that little extra."

One way to tell a good candidate, the recruiters say, is by listening to the stories they tell during the interview process.

"I love it when they get emotional," Janda said. "They get it."

Nurses in critical care areas such as intensive care units approach their jobs, patients and families differently from nurses who see patients for well-child visits.

Some employees thrive on seeing lots of different families for short periods; others like to form long-term connections.

Hospital recruiters say it's equally important for employees with no direct patient care to have a connection with the children. They ask Information Technology candidates, for instance, whether they realize that their jobs — programming computers, installing software — are about taking care of the kids. Doctors, patients and parents are all counting on that technology.

Dr. O'Donnell likes to tell people that the employees of Children's Mercy are his heroes for their commitment, their dedication, their love of children and the work they do. All those things and more, he said, made him humble and proud to call them co-workers. The 2006 report to the Robert Wood Johnson Foundation on the hospital's cultural transformation cited one of the keys in human resources:

> *View all employees as essential contributors to success, rather than commodities.*

The report contrasted the Children's Mercy way of operating with a traditional business philosophy: "Those at the top decide. Those in the middle direct. Those at the bottom do."

"Great corporations have operated successfully under its approach," the report acknowledged. "But does it build leaders that can take a stagnant organization and help it reach seemingly unachievable new levels?

"Children's Mercy didn't think so and, as a result, began a process in the mid-1990s that shifted how employees and the organization related to each other. The process was neither smooth nor easy, as each part of the equation had to overcome long-held notions of role and responsibilities.

"Yet today, this evolution has created an environment where turnover is down, where certain jobs categories have waiting lists and where many who leave the organization for greener pastures end up returning."

One example of this new approach involved the creation of "co-manager" positions in some of the patient care areas where jobs were hard to keep filled, in part because of stress and long hours. Although there were risks to the co-manager concept — higher costs of employing two managers instead of one, or confusion among the staff if the co-managers made conflicting decisions — a study in one unit showed that it worked.

For the benefit of the hospital, turnover was reduced. For the benefit of managers, work-life balance was achieved. And staff had increased access to its leaders. One of the early co-managers put it this way: "You can work and have a life. It's been a real plus for me, my family and Children's Mercy."

As the hospital, recruitment of the medical staff was a crucial ingredient. With a national shortage of pediatric specialists, Children's Mercy often competes with other children's hospitals across the country for the best talent. Vicki Clarke, the director of physician recruitment, said the growing reputation of Children's Mercy as a place that truly put kids first had helped set it apart.

"Our candidates hear the message: Everything we do, we do for the kids," she said.

Most of the candidates for physician jobs — Clarke has been recruiting 45 new doctors a year for several years — have had some previous connection to Children's Mercy. Either they knew someone at the hospital, or they did part of their training there.

One thing that attracts them, she said, is the team approach with nursing, the behavioral and developmental sciences, family-centered and psychosocial care.

"We don't have trouble recruiting doctors. Our staff has a good reputation nationally, as does the hospital."

Getting the right employees in the door is one important step. Having them embrace the culture comes next.

Integration with the medical staff

Denise Dowd, MD, an emergency medicine and injury-prevention specialist, knows the difference between how nurses and doctors are trained. She went to nursing school before deciding to become a physician.

Nurses, she said, are taught to think in a holistic way, to look at different influences on children's health and their illness. They consider living conditions and family structure and emotional, spiritual and psychological influences. They learn to ask about nutrition and safety. They design care plans that are circular, that encompass every bit of patients' lives.

Doctors, for the most part, have a different approach. They are taught to look at their task this way: a healthy child encounters an illness, disease or accident. That makes the child ill or injured. The doctor intervenes, perhaps with medicine. Soon, the child is back to being healthy. For the doctors, the process is linear.

Dr. Daryl Lynch, who led the Adolescent Medicine Section at Children's Mercy for many years before retiring in 2018, said doctors were smart, strong-willed individuals who were often trained as if they were going into practice by themselves.

"A lot of doctors are like farmers," Dr. Lynch said. "They want to be independent. They want to be on their own. But we can't do it alone anymore."

"Doctors need to stay out of the way and let (the psychosocial professionals) do their jobs," said Dr. Mike Artman, MD, chairman of the Department of Pediatrics at Children's Mercy. "It starts with the nursing staff. We can and should support it."

One of the things driving increased support among doctors is growing scientific evidence of the mind-body connection. Dr. Artman, who is a cardiologist, said a study of children who had heart surgery showed that one in five had symptoms of post-traumatic stress disorder.

"There is literature out there that shows being in the hospital can be bad," Dr. Artman said. "We know that a comforting environment is better. We know facility design helps. We know we can promote resilience and that helps healing.

"Doctors aren't driving psychosocial care, but we can certainly support it so it can grow and grow, and we can care for the whole patient and not just the disease."

Dr. Lynch did his medical residency at Children's Mercy in the late 1980s. Although there was already a variety of psychosocial support when he arrived, he recalls, it was not seen as a part of the medical staff's jobs. Because he was interested in working with teenagers, he sought grants for issues like teen pregnancy prevention and substance abuse. These issues were not normally discussed in the context of a children's hospital.

"Some other doctors scoffed at this," recalled Dr. Lynch, who in 2018 was the associate chair of pediatrics at Children's Mercy. "They didn't think I was a 'real doctor' — 'What are you, a social worker?'

"No, but we look at the whole person. You can't separate the mind and the body. I knew if I am going to make a difference in teens' lives, this is what we need to do."

Dr. Lynch tells the story of one teen patient suffering from seizures. Other doctors saw her and ordered a variety of tests. They couldn't figure it out. But once he began to work with the teen, by getting to know more about her personally, by listening to her, learning about her home and school life, he discovered her deep, dark secret. A janitor at school was abusing her.

Removed from the situation and encouraged to continue to talk about it and confront her emotions, her physical health improved. The seizures disappeared.

"This is science," Dr. Lynch says. "It's good science."

Many pediatricians are already inclined this way. Medical students who decide to specialize in pediatrics know they are going to be working with not only their patients, but also their parents. That's a given and may be one of the reasons that children's hospitals have been early adopters of psychosocial care and patient- and family-centered practices.

The American Academy of Pediatrics says, "when you're a general pediatrician, you're a member of every family you take care of."

According to a study in the journal *Medical Education,* most doctors leave medical school more "doctor- or disease-centered" and more paternalistic than when they entered. But separate research by Children's Mercy found that the pediatric residents in its program bucked that trend. Most residents at Children's Mercy perceived themselves, and were perceived by families, as patient- and family-centered at the beginning of their residency and remained that way throughout.

Pediatricians have chosen a profession pioneered by Abraham Jacobi, who urged doctors to become child advocates and who understood that care extended beyond the walls of the hospital.

One of the early adopters on the medical staff was Dr. Jay Portnoy. In the late 1990s, Dr. Portnoy, chief of Asthma, Allergy and Immunology, noticed that he was repeatedly seeing children who were not getting better. He decided to look beyond the diagnosis, the prescribed treatment and the clinic walls.

"What was going on outside where the kids were living their lives?" he asked. He and a team developed a set of best-practice guidelines for treating asthma patients. The new guidelines included education for community pediatricians who saw those patients before the Children's Mercy doctors, and for the patients and families themselves, who were on the front lines of the disease.

The team developed Asthma Action Cards, which are basically treatment plans and sets of instructions on flash cards given to children and their parents. Easily understood, the cards are customized for each patient, family and environment.

The cards, along with training provided by Children's Mercy staff to the staff in private medical practices, led to a reduction of about 50 percent in emergency room visits and hospitalizations for these asthma patients. The program also generated revenue; insurance plans directed patients to Children's Mercy because costly hospitalization could be avoided by focusing on causes of the disease, not just treatment.

In addition, Dr. Portnoy's group launched an environmental assessment team, which visits patient homes to inspect living conditions that could contribute to a child's symptoms. Depending on what a team discovers in the homes, it can provide cleaning supplies, a vacuum cleaner and perhaps even some money for new heating and air conditioning. The Children's Mercy team has also been called into public schools to help with mold and other environmental problems.

Both programs continue. The environmental health program has led to the publication of national best-practice guidelines for environmental control. Similar programs have been implemented at hospitals in Dallas, Memphis and elsewhere across the country, according to the Children's Hospital Association.

"By taking information and education directly to families and building partnerships with community organizations, children's hospitals are making strides in reducing asthma admission and helping kids breathe easier," the association said in a news release in October 2017.

Another medical staff member who is a staunch believer in family-centered and psychosocial care is Dr. Warady. As chief of Nephrology at Children's Mercy, Dr. Warady has worked for years, if not decades, with children on dialysis or in need of a kidney transplant. It's impossible to ignore the importance of the family in a child's care, he said.

"If we ask them to do something to help their child and it's not that they won't, but that they *can't* do it, then it's not going to work," he says. "We have to recognize they have lives outside of here."

Dr. Warady arrived at Children's Mercy in the early 1980s as a resident. Even then, he said, the team approach to care was coming into practice. As medicine became more complex and as parents were asked to take on more and more responsibility for their children's care, family-centered aspects of treatment grew in importance.

By its nature, family-centered care involves care outside the walls of the hospital and the doctors' offices. No longer can doctors think in straight lines.

"This type of individualized care is not easy," Dr. Warady said. "It takes work and commitment from both sides. ... The benefits of the time spent become apparent as families recognize our commitment to work with them as partners and not merely as patients or 'customers.'

"Taking care of kids is a team sport," he said. "The stronger the family and the more support we can give them, the better they will do."

Behavioral health specialists are part of the team. Although child psychologists have been on the Children's Mercy staff since the 1980s, they were not then fully integrated into medical teams. Mental health has long been treated as distinct from physical health, despite growing evidence that the two are inseparable. That began to change in 1994, when a psychologist was hired to work exclusively with patients in Hematology/Oncology. The benefits of having a mental health professional as an active, full-time member of the medical team became apparent.

Other sections soon began hiring their own psychologists to address issues specific to their own patients' psychosocial challenges. By 2018, about half of the 50 psychologists on staff at Children's Mercy were working directly with medical teams for children with chronic diseases (nephrology, gastroenterology and so on) to care for their unique challenges.

Dr. Sarah Soden, a developmental pediatrician and chief of the section of Developmental and Behavioral Sciences, said that when she did her residency in the late 1990s the integration of mental health with the rest of the health team was well underway.

"Behavioral health *is* health care," she said. "We get that here."

Additional training for physicians

One of the ways to get better is to offer new doctors experience with families.

"This isn't something necessarily taught in medical school or read about in a medical journal," Dr. Warady said. "It's an important development learned firsthand from patients and families over the years."

With that understanding, Children's Mercy has introduced practices to help train the next generation of pediatricians in how to treat the whole child.

Each July, a new class of several dozen pediatric residents joins the staff at Children's Mercy. These residents, having just completed medical school, know a lot about biology, anatomy and disease. A big part of their residency training is learning how to care for children "in the real world." And that means understanding the psychosocial needs of children under their care, needs they won't glean from a textbook.

In their orientation to Children's Mercy, residents meet with members of the Family and Teen Advisory boards.

"This informal lunch begins the process of removing barriers between resident physicians and the family and allows residents the opportunity to hear about parent experiences," said Dr. Emily Goodwin, a pediatrician in the Beacon Program, a medical home for children with complex conditions. She helps direct the family-centered care curriculum for residents.

A major part of the curriculum, she said, involves home visits that all residents complete. The young doctors are paired with a family that is familiar with Children's Mercy and that has at least one child with special health care needs.

"The home visits allow the resident to see the 'normalcy' of these family's challenging lives," Dr. Goodwin said. "Residents are able to recognize the impact that medical technology and their recommendations have in real life, as well as the obstacles and joys that these families face on a daily basis."

After those visits, residents meet with the Patient and Family Engagement Program managers, who are parents on staff, to debrief and to reflect on how the experience will affect their future practice of medicine.

Residents further attend a panel discussion called "What Mattered Most," where parents talk to residents about their experience of having a child who died and what mattered most to them during the child's hospitalization and treatment. The residents take part in daily family-centered rounds on the inpatient units where parents are a part of the team making decisions. They also join Home Care therapists to see patients and families in their homes and visit food pantries and public assistance sites to better understand the experiences of their families. To further enhance patient and family engagement, residents and parents also work together on a quality improvement project.

"Each experience is designed to help residents better understand medicine from the patients' perspective, opening the door for improved communication and hopefully improved information and decision sharing in future encounters," Dr. Goodwin said.

Providing good care requires good communication and trusting relationships among doctors, patients and families. Children's Mercy is designing training materials to help doctors quickly establish rapport. The expertise and experience of Child Life specialists will be crucial to this training.

As early as 1987, there were calls for increased attention to communication in medical education. The *Journal of Medical Education* proposed that "from the beginning of their professional education, medical students need assistance in

What is family?

There's the proverb that "It Takes a Village" to raise a child. You could also say, "It Takes a Family," and that is why Children's Mercy is a strong advocate of family-centered care. Families provide most of the care for their children. And because they know their children better than the staff at Children's Mercy ever will, the hospital leadership believes it is important to provide them information and support.

What, then, is a family? The Institute for Patient- and Family-Centered Care adopted the following definition from a Task Force on Young Children and Families of the New Mexico Legislature:

"Families are big, small, extended, nuclear, multi-generational, with one parent, two parents and grandparents. We live under one roof or many. A family can be as temporary as a few weeks or as permanent as forever. We become part of a family by birth, adoption, marriage or from a desire for mutual support. ... A family is a culture unto itself, with different values and unique ways of realizing its dream; together our families become the source of our rich cultural heritage and spiritual diversity. ... Our families create neighborhoods, communities, states and nations."

building their interpersonal skills and developing a patient-centered rather than a disease-centered approach to care."

Dr. Lynch, the adolescent medicine specialist, said much could be done to help physicians be better listeners.

"We can teach people to smile, to say hello," he said. "I always tell young doctors, 'Sit down.' That sends a message." He also suggests doctors sit at eye level or below the patients and family to convey a relationship of partnership, not power. "Body language is so important."

The power of words is also considered.

"There can be a difference between what a health care provider says and what the family actually hears," said Sheryl Chadwick, a patient and family engagement program manager and mother of a former patient.

Some words or phrases that can elicit a negative response:
- "You need a break."
- "As soon as possible ..."
- "It's our policy ..."
- "There's nothing more we can do."

On the other hand, words that can shift attitudes toward the positive:
- "What I can do is ..."
- "Tell me about your child."
- "What usually works for your child?"

Communication is also emphasized in working with language interpreters. In 1998, Children's Mercy established a formal Language Services Department to help staff overcome language barriers with families with limited proficiency in English. In 2017, the staff served as the voice of more than 58,000 patients and their families, in more than 100 languages. There are interpreters on staff to help with the most common non-English languages among the patients (Spanish, Arabic, Somali, Burmese and Vietnamese). The hospital also uses a service to provide other in-person interpreters and a phone or video service for languages encountered less frequently.

"We can all empathize with the anxiety a parent [with] limited English ... must feel when unable to clearly communicate with clinical providers," said Kathy S. Smith, director of Language and Disability Services at Children's Mercy. "These services are vital to safe health outcomes, promoting a positive patient experience and reducing health care disparities."

Another part of the residents' education puts new doctors in the role of advocate, as envisioned by the founder of modern pediatrics, Dr. Abraham Jacobi.

All second-year residents at Children's Mercy take part in the month-long Community Health and Advocacy rotation. One of the goals of the rotation is to instill the idea that every pediatrician should be a child advocate. One exercise is writing a letter to the editor of the local newspaper focusing on a child health topic. In the 2016-17 academic year, letters from 11 Children's Mercy residents were published in *The Kansas City Star.*

Dr. Molly Krager, a pediatric hospitalist, helps organize the advocacy rotation.

"It would be nearly impossible for a pediatrician to go through his or her career without encountering an opportunity to advocate for a patient in some way," Dr. Krager said. Efforts can range from helping a single hungry child access food stamps, to writing a letter to the editor about an issue that affects the well-being of all children in a community, to advocating for all children in the state or the country.

The work, Dr. Krager noted, helps doctors understand how outside forces — psychosocial forces, if you will — can threaten the health of children.

"Pediatricians are uniquely qualified to be advocates," she said. "They work on the front lines and are able to observe trends and identify needs within a patient population; they are trained to critically appraise literature and identify evidence-based approaches, and they serve as respected members of the community with powerful voices."

The American Academy of Pediatrics also supports doctors as advocates. The academy's "Definition of a Pediatrician" policy statement ends this way: "A pediatrician participates at the community level in preventing or solving problems in child health care and publicly advocates the causes of children."

Medical education at Children's Mercy also routinely includes formal "grand round" presentations in the areas of psychosocial care and advocacy. Grand rounds are formal meetings or lectures for physicians to discuss clinical cases, research and other educational components.

Another vital piece of the medical education program includes an introduction to Child Life. When the introduction was first proposed, medical education staff balked; they thought it would be too time-consuming and believed the young doctors already knew about Child Life. But the Child Life specialists persisted and got the opportunity to pilot a program.

Referred to as boot camp, the program uses games and role-playing to focus on child development theory (including a lighthearted "Piaget Rap" video), health care play and procedure preparation. Boot camp is presented monthly to a select group of residents as part of their education in behavioral and developmental science.

Residents are taught about common stressors for children and strategies for comforting and distracting them such as watching movies or cartoons, blowing bubbles, asking questions or simply holding hands. For many new doctors, the introduction to Child Life is eye-opening.

"Child Life is significantly more involved with the patient care than I previously thought," one resident wrote in his course evaluation. "Also, it was great to see how Child Life can fully explain a procedure such as an IV using a doll with an actual IV attached. I believe this is a critical and very useful aspect to patient care and should be used by all patients."

Another resident commented: "Awesome experience. I didn't realize how much more I could be offering to patients."

Pre- and post-boot camp surveys show the impact of the program. When asked whether they knew the stages of child development before boot camp, 55 percent of residents said they did. Afterward 87 percent said so. In addition, after class, 100 percent of residents said procedure preparation was important, that Child Life had a sizable impact on helping children cope with stressful events and that health care play helped increase a child's understanding of his or her diagnosis.

Guided by a few of their own pioneers, along with education, practice and a growing body of scientific evidence, the medical staff at Children's Mercy has come to embrace psychosocial care as essential in the treatment for children. Koenig, in Patient and Family Support Services, said parents *wanted* doctors who were experts on disease and who were laser-focused on that illness. But parents also wanted the team to care for the emotional and social aspects of life, she said. That might not be the expertise of the doctors but that was OK.

Doctors traditionally have been seen as the "head" of the medical team, Dr. Artman said, but the tables have shifted and a true partnership has developed.

"Some doctors have a fighter-pilot mentality: go it alone," he continued. "But what we really need are wing men."

Another initiative that calls on all employees to embrace family-centered and psychosocial care is the drive to make Children's Mercy a "trauma-informed" institution. That begins by recognizing that almost everyone who comes in contact with Children's Mercy has been affected by trauma — a terrible accident or disease, an unexpected or untimely death, violence in the home or in the community.

Trauma-informed means understanding what's going on beneath the surface in the life of the patient and the family. Trauma can be physical or psychological and affects everyone differently. Addressing a family's unique circumstances can improve care, and families who feel they are in a safe and supportive place are easier to work with.

No one is immune to the impact of trauma and trauma affects everything: how we feel, how we cope, how we approach and respond to medical care and how we heal.

Role of families takes root

Parents form an equal part of the team. They spend many more hours with their children than do doctors, or even the nurses who are at bedsides their entire shifts. As technology expands the possibilities of in-home care and the cost of inpatient care soars, parents are key to their children's health.

Children's Mercy today is proud of the role that parents play, not only in the care of their children but also in the operation of the hospital. Recognizing that families face different challenges depending on the part of the institution doing the treatment, there are more than 10 family advisory boards. Their focuses range from children with food allergies and rare diseases to those with inflammatory bowel disease and heart problems. There is an advisory board for Spanish-speaking families (which helps acknowledge their unique cultural and language circumstances) and three boards for patients themselves. The Teen Advisory Board was the first Patient and Family Advisory Committee, established in 1998.

The hospital has not always been so family-centric. As late as the 1980s, parents were considered visitors and asked to leave at night. Many doctors and nurses thought parents and siblings got in the way of healing, instead of playing an important part in it. Some doctors did little listening. They were in charge.

That began to change, little by little. In the late 1980s a parent was invited to help redecorate the floor where cancer patients were treated. In the 1990s, three parents were invited to join the Patient Care and Family Environment Committee. In the early 2000s, that became the first Family Advisory Board.

Once the door was opened for parents, they came streaming in, eager to provide a new perspective and help improve the care for others like themselves. Not all of them were volunteers. In 2006, Children's Mercy hired its first parent on staff, Ginny Miller, whose daughter had been treated there for years.

Kaylee Hurt, a mom whose daughter, Kaydee, a micro-preemie, spent months in the Neonatal Intensive Care Unit, joined the Children's Mercy staff in 2017 (when Kaydee was 4) to help support other parents in the NICU.

Hers is a new position, and not everyone on staff understands or appreciates her role. There is mutual respect. Hurt stays out of the doctors' way and they give her the space she needs. She knows from experience how important it is to have someone to talk to who has been in your situation.

"It's terrifying," she said of having a baby in the NICU. She said her experience helped her relate to other new moms who were just as frightened. "I tell them, I know what it's like to live in that chair."

Hurt meets with each family who comes into the NICU and offers parenting classes and support groups. Mostly, though, she offers them the comfort of someone who has been there.

"The health of the parents is just as important as the health of the child," she said. "We need to take care of all of them."

Other parents on staff include Cheryl Chadwick and DeeJo Miller, who started working at Children's Mercy in 2008. They take part in orientation for new patient-care employees so the new staff see how seriously the role of the parents is taken at Children's Mercy.

"No one chooses to come to Children's Mercy because no one chooses to have a sick child," Chadwick said. "But I remember the first nurse I met who said, 'I'm sorry you're here, but we're going to help you with this journey.'"

For Chadwick, that meant helping her son, Kyle, who was 6 when he was diagnosed with leukemia. During his three-and-a-half years of chemotherapy, Kyle had many complications. He spent 104 days as an inpatient, made trip after trip to the Emergency Room, had 24 surgeries and was seen by more than 20 specialists. In 2016, he graduated from the University of Kansas School of Nursing and in 2018 was working as a surgical nurse.

As part of the hospital's ethics program, Chadwick and Miller present a tutorial called "This is My Child, This is Your Patient," which is designed to explain how parents and doctors are coming from distinctive points of view. They concentrate on empathy, communication and understanding. To help put their audience into a parent's shoes, they start with an activity that includes handing everyone an envelope.

"Please don't open it," Chadwick tells the new staffers. "First, think about an important child in your life. It might be your child or grandchild, a niece or a nephew. ... Write that child's name on the envelope. Take a minute to think about the hopes and dreams you have for this child. What special memory do you have? ... What do you think they'll be like when they grow up?"

The audience then opens the envelopes. Inside is a slip of paper with a medical condition written on it.

"Imagine for a moment that the child whose name is on that envelope experiences the condition on that slip of paper," Miller said. "How do you feel? What are you thinking? How will this affect those hopes and dreams you have for this child and the rest of their family? What's on your calendar for next week? What will have to be rearranged to come back to Children's Mercy?

"You don't get to choose what would be inside your envelope and you can't trade with your neighbor."

The audience sits in silence. The parents' perspective becomes clearer. Real life meets the practice of medicine.

"As you know, every day there are families who come to Children's Mercy and are handed an envelope."

For Miller, the envelope was for her daughter, Hannah, who in 2004 was 13 years old and a junior Olympian when she was diagnosed with Stage IV Burkitt's lymphoma. After a bone marrow transplant, 18 months of treatment and more than 300 inpatient days, Hannah went home to recover. She graduated from college and got married. On September 7, 2016, the 12-year anniversary of her cancer diagnosis, she gave birth to a healthy baby girl. Her journey changed many, many lives.

Chadwick and Miller help organize the family advisory boards and serve on many hospital committees. In the decade they have been on staff, their positions have gone from something of a novelty to an essential part of hospital operations. They are called on throughout the organization to give the parents' perspective. They have been instrumental in the hospital's safety, quality and design work.

Among the benefits to the organization — and the care it provides — are challenging the status quo, offering a fresh perspective and ensuring that the staff makes fewer assumptions about patient and family needs.

"You will never meet a family here on their best days," Miller said.

At orientation, Chadwick and Miller explain the core concepts of family-centered care: information sharing, participation and collaboration, and respect and dignity.

"We are not here to overwhelm the parents. We want them to participate at the level they choose," Chadwick said. "Families don't have to change themselves to be cared for here. We meet them where they are."

Tying it all together

With doctors, families and people from across the institution working together, family-centered and psychosocial care is quite an operation at Children' Mercy. In 2017, the hospital brought many of the services together under one administrative umbrella. The goal was to avoid duplication, improve efficiency and bring a strategic focus to the various components of the care.

Heather Brungardt, a social worker by training, was named administrative director of the Division of Psychosocial Services. Brungardt said she and her team are motivated by a quote from one of the hospital's founders, Dr. Katharine Berry

Richardson:

"Skill cannot take the place of sympathy and understanding, for science without heart is ugly and pitiless."

In all, there are about 320 people in the Division of Psychosocial Services. The three main departments – Chaplaincy, Social Work and Child Life – require an investment of about $13 million a year from the hospital. That's about 1 percent of the total budget. There is no direct reimbursement from either private insurance or Medicaid. A few small grants pay some of the bills. And while hospital financial officers are paying close attention to the bottom line everywhere, the commitment to psychosocial services remains strong.

"There is widej acknowledgment that psychosocial services add value to our care," said David Cauble, executive vice president and chief financial officer. "It may not be realized through reimbursement, but we know it provides tremendous value to the children."

Dr. Warady, the nephrologist, wrote in 2017: "Do their contributions as integral members of the chronic care team make a difference? I can state without any reservation that my fulfillment as a physician and my goal to always provide the highest level of patient care would be compromised without them."

In the first place, Cauble said, doctors, nurses and everyone at Children's Mercy are there not just to treat illness and fix sick bodies, but also to *serve*. He pointed to an article by Rachel Naomi Remen, MD, associate clinical professor of Family and Community Medicine at the University of California-San Francisco Medical School. Its title: "Helping, Fixing or Serving."

"Fixing and helping create a distance between people, but we cannot serve at a distance. We can only serve that to which we are profoundly connected. Helping, fixing and serving represent three different ways of seeing life. When you help, you see life as weak. When you fix, you see life as broken. When you serve, you see life as whole.

"Fixing and helping may be the work of the ego, and service the work of the soul. Service rests on the premise that the nature of life is sacred, that life is a holy mystery which has an unknown purpose. When we serve, we know that we belong to life and to that purpose."

Managing psychosocial care

Meeting the needs of children takes a lot of people with special skills. But the more people, equipment and the administrative departments are involved, the more complicated the process becomes. More proverbial silos are constructed.

Silos are good for storing grain. But caring for children with complex medical and psychosocial needs? Not so much. Children's Mercy did something about that.

In years past, the administrative structure of Children's Mercy had psychosocial services reporting to various executive vice presidents. That was by design. Dr. O'Donnell wanted each executive vice president to be intimately involved with some aspect of psychosocial care so he or she would be both knowledgeable and invested in its success.

For instance, Chief Operating Officer Jo Stueve, who came up through the managed care field, and Chief Administrative Officer Sandra A.J. Lawrence, a former chief financial officer, initially did not have a working knowledge of psychosocial services. But with chaplains, social workers and others reporting to them and advocating for their work and their patients, the executives saw the big picture. Soon, the entire executive team was championing the value of psychosocial care, not just one senior administrator.

That helped psychosocial care became more ingrained in the culture and accepted throughout Children's Mercy. Yet another problem arose. As care, regulatory requirements and the organization itself became more complex, the need grew for better coordination and accountability among physicians, nurses, departments, specialties, buildings and psychosocial services.

"Parents have told us some of our processes are confusing and uncoordinated," said Heather Brungardt, senior administrative director of Psychosocial Services. "We can fix that with better coordination and planning."

Beginning in 2014, hospital leaders began working on smoothing out the problem. That led to the creation in 2017 of two new administrative structures: the Division of Psychosocial Services and the Department of Care Continuum.

Brungardt, a social worker by training, would oversee the Division of Psychosocial Services, which includes:

- Social work, including ambulatory and primary care medical social work, home visitation programs and child and family mental health services
- Child Life
- Spiritual services, including the Lisa Barth Chapel.
- Language services
- Patient advocates

- Children's Mercy Operation Breakthrough Health Clinic
- Parent support programs
- Music therapy
- Hospital-based school teachers
- Kreamer Resource Center for Families.

Brungardt, like other advocates of psychosocial services, is quick to emphasize the medical and business value of her teams' work. At a meeting with medical staff in the summer of 2018, she presented data and anecdotes to make her case. One doctor, who was not part of the Division of Psychosocial Services, helped make Brungardt's point for her.

"Psychosocial care plays a critically important role in the Children's Mercy emergency departments," said Gregory Conners, MD, director of the Division of Emergency Medicine until 2019. "Medical social workers and chaplains provide family assessments, counseling and resources. Every day, patients with behavioral health needs rely on the presence of the Acute Mental Health Services team of social workers. Interpreters allow for effective communication with non-English speaking patients.

"We love our psychosocial services and so do our patients and families."

As for the other division, a big part of the work of the Department of Care Continuum, under the direction of Ma'ata Hardman, is what used to be called "discharge planning," the work involved in dismissing children from the hospital and sending them home with instructions for care, follow-up appointments and more. Today, that's known as "care coordination." Hardman's teams and Brungardt's group work closely together, along with the nursing and medical staffs of the hospital and families.

The new administrative structure under Hardman's watch brings together:

- Physicians, nurses, departments, specialties, buildings and psychosocial services
- Inpatient nurse-care management and social work.
- Primary care nurse-care management and coordination
- Home-care and clinical-care teams in the hospital's Pediatric Care Network, which are responsible for patients who are part of Missouri and Kansas Medicaid programs.
- The Blue Valley School District collaboration with social workers.

"Our mission is to optimize and align care," Hardman said.

And it seems to be working. In the year after Care Continuum was created, the average length of stay by patients served by the division dropped 35 percent. Readmission rates dropped 10 percent.

CHAPTER 6

Translating science into health

One thing that complicates widespread adoption of psychosocial care, especially among medical and other professionals, is the lack of scientific evidence of its impact and importance. But in the last 10 years particularly, a growing body of data has emerged that supports how important both nature and nurturing are to the development of healthy children and adults.

"We can't ignore the science," said Dr. Dowd, an emergency medicine specialist at Children's Mercy.

A groundbreaking study in the late 1990s by Kaiser Permanente showed that early childhood events could affect health over a lifetime. Known today as the ACE Study, for Adverse Childhood Experiences, it showed that, the more adversity to which children were exposed, the more health problems they would have and the shorter lives they would live.

The initiative for the study came from Dr. Vincent Felitti, who in the 1980s was trying to figure out why some patients he was treating with a new liquid diet would first lose weight and then put it back on. He discovered that some of the patients had been abused as children and it led him to wonder whether having a rough childhood could affect health.

The ACE study found a relationship between childhood trauma and the chances of a serious illness or health condition later in life. Although not a direct cause-and-effect relationship, it was hard to ignore the association. Hundreds more studies followed and today it is widely agreed that childhood trauma and the accompanying toxic stress have lifetime implications. One study from 2018 suggested a connection between early trauma and dementia in rats that may translate to humans.

Some believe that the mere act of talking about trauma can help reduce some of its effects. A National Public Radio report in 2015 carried the headline "Can Family Secrets Make You Sick?"

If doctors know not only how their patients are sick, but also why they are sick, Dr. Felitti said, outcomes can be improved.

In 2014, the American Academy of Pediatrics launched the Center on Healthy Resilient Children to help children with toxic stress.

Adverse Childhood Experiences are defined as:

- Physical abuse
- Sexual abuse
- Emotional abuse
- Physical neglect
- Emotional neglect
- Exposure to domestic violence
- Substance misuse in the household
- Mental illness in the household
- Parental separation or divorce
- Incarcerated household member
- Living in an unsafe neighborhood
- Witnessing violence in the neighborhood

Although all children and adults have stress in their lives, these ACEs are particularly dangerous. Studies show that exposure to four or more ACEs can increase the likelihood of heart disease and stroke by more than 200 percent, depression by 460 percent and suicide by as much as 1,220 percent.

One of the leading national voices on reducing ACEs is Dr. Nadine Burke Harris. Working in a pediatric clinic in a low-income area of San Francisco, she saw children she knew were living with high "doses" of adversity and she could see the evidence: trauma was affecting their developing brains and also their growing bodies.

"Does it seem like a difficult problem to solve? Yes," Dr. Harris told *The New York Times* in 2016. "Does it seem harder than cancer? I don't know. Medicine and public health are all about solving hard problems."

Harris, in a Technology, Entertainment and Design (TED) Talk in 2014, explained some of the brain science involved:

> Some people looked at this data and they said: "Come on. You have a rough childhood, you're more likely to drink and smoke and do all these things that are going to ruin your health. This isn't science. This is just bad behavior."
>
> It turns out this is exactly where the science comes in. We now understand better than ever how exposure to early adversity affects the developing brains and bodies of children. It affects areas like the *nucleus accumbens*, the pleasure and reward center of the brain that is implicated in substance dependence. It inhibits the prefrontal cortex,

which is necessary for impulse control and executive function, a critical area for learning. And on MRI scans, we see measurable differences in the amygdala, the brain's fear response center.

So there are real neurologic reasons why individuals exposed to high doses of adversity are more likely to engage in high-risk behavior, and that's important to know.

But it turns out that even if you don't engage in any high-risk behavior, you're still more likely to develop heart disease or cancer.

While some stress is good, we know too much of it is a bad thing. And now there is scientific proof.

Again, from Harris' TED Talk:

Well, imagine you're walking in the forest and you see a bear. Immediately, your hypothalamus sends a signal to your pituitary, which sends a signal to your adrenal gland that says, "Release stress hormones! Adrenaline! Cortisol!" And so your heart starts to pound, your pupils dilate, your airways open up, and you are ready to either fight that bear or run from the bear. And that is wonderful if you're in a forest and there's a bear. But the problem is, What happens when the bear comes home every night, and this system is activated over and over and over again, and it goes from being adaptive, or life-saving, to maladaptive, or health-damaging? Children are especially sensitive to this repeated stress activation, because their brains and bodies are just developing. High doses of adversity not only affect brain structure and function, they affect the developing immune system, developing hormonal systems, and even the way our DNA is read and transcribed.

Toxic stress literally gets under your skin and changes your DNA.

The American Academy of Pediatrics is advocating routine screening of children for adversity. The AAP knows doctors are not the only ones needed to address this issue. In a policy statement from its Committee on Psychosocial Aspects of Child and Family Health, the group calls for a fundamental shift in the way the general public and policymakers view and invest in early childhood.

In 2016, Children's Mercy did just that with the first Child Health Summit. The meeting pulled together more than 150 representatives from community organizations to assess health needs. The No. 1 problem, the group voted, was childhood poverty and its related adversity. Children's Mercy and the AAP know it will take multiple partners, such as government and charitable and social service agencies, to alleviate these societal problems.

Although science is leading to a consensus about the problem, the solution is not simple. Yet there is agreement that the kind of psychosocial and family-centered care being practiced by Children's Mercy and others is a start.

One such helpful program is Team for Infants Exposed to Substance Abuse — TIES. Since 1990, this program has worked with moms who have been drug users, who are trying to turn their lives around, and who have or are about to have infants. Children's Mercy workers meet with families in their homes to provide support and information, to help build a strong bond between parents and baby, to overcome barriers to health care and to connect families to other community services. Hundreds of parents and children have been a part of TIES through the nearly 30 years of the program at Children's Mercy.

"When I enrolled in TIES, I didn't have a place to live, my kids had been removed from my home and my life was a total mess," one mom said. "TIES specialists guide you and you can and want to do it on your own. They are your cheerleaders. With TIES support and my perseverance, I was able to get my G.E.D., graduated from a community college and am currently attending a four-year university on a full scholarship. I'm happy to say that I now have a place to live, my kids are back in my home and my life is on track!"

A similar program available to a broader group is Healthy Families Children's Mercy, a partner of Health Families America. In this program, experts help families by promoting bonding and teaching parenting skills with the guiding belief that early, nurturing relationships are the foundation for lifelong health development. Healthy Families America reports reduced levels of harsh parenting, neglect and physical and psychological abuse in families using the program. According to the HFA, the program helps improve children's school performances and prevents ACEs.

By working with children to reduce their stress and with families to understand and help with social conditions, Children's Mercy is beginning to address some of the social and psychological issues that can cause problems later. Yet there is much more work to be done.

In its technical report, "The Lifelong Effects of Early Childhood Adversity and Toxic Stress," the American Academy of Pediatrics saw the challenges as great, just as it saw the potential rewards.

"This converging, multi-disciplinary science of human development," the report said, "has profound implications for our ability to enhance the life prospects of children and to strengthen the social and economic fabric of society."

The stigma of mental health

Mental health problems are real. The stigma is strong. The negative implications powerful. Those with mental illness might be called "crazy." If they commit crimes, they may be labeled "monsters." With medical conditions there is sympathy; with a mental disease, there is shame and guilt.

Mental health and mental illness are complex and there is much we do not understand about them. Some in the health care industry suggest dealing with emotions and mental health is somehow less important than heart conditions, cancer or kidney disease. But with the surge in suicides and mass shootings tied to mental illness in the national consciousness, that argument seems less convincing.

National statistics on the impact and prevalence of mental illness are attention-grabbing:

- The number of children admitted to children's hospitals for thoughts of suicide or self-harm has more than doubled in the last decade.
- The use of anti-depression medication rose 65 percent in the 15 years before 2017.
- Serious mental illness costs the United States $192.2 million a year.
- More than 20 percent of youth aged 13 to 18 experience a severe mental disorder at some time. For children aged 8-15, the estimate is 13 percent.
- Seventy percent of people in juvenile justice systems have at least one mental health condition and at least 20 percent live with a serious mental illness.
- Slightly more than half of children ages 8 to 15 and with a mental health condition receive mental health services in a year.
- Mood disorders, including major depression, dysthymic disorder and bipolar disorder are the third most common cause of hospitalization in the United States for both youth and adults aged 18 to 44.
- Adults with serious mental illness die an average 25 years earlier than others, largely because of treatable medical conditions.
- Suicide is the 10th leading cause of death in the United States, the third leading cause of death for people ages 10 to 14 and the second leading cause of death for those aged 15 to 24.
- More than 90 percent of children who die by suicide have a mental-health condition.

At Children's Mercy and other hospitals across the country, these chilling statistics are not being ignored. Finding solutions has proved elusive. But not for lack of trying.

"As medical science has grown, mental health has lagged," said Dr. Mike

Artman, chair of pediatrics at Children's Mercy. "There is so much we know about the pathology of diseases ... but we still don't know much about how the brain works."

Dr. Lynch, an adolescent medicine specialist, put it this way: "The brain is the last frontier. Because we don't understand it, it tends to be shunned, under-studied or perhaps worse, stigmatized."

The problem is not unique in the history of medicine. Consider epilepsy, which thousands of years ago was considered, even in the medical world, to be the result of evil or occult influences and its sufferers were shunned. Leprosy is another ancient disease that resulted in negative stigmas and isolation for those who were afflicted. Fast forward to the 20th century and there were some who suggested the equivalent of "leper colonies" for those who had AIDS.

"Sometimes if we don't understand it, if we can't see it, we shove it off into the corner," Dr. Artman said.

Doctors are trained to help people. They ask questions and they often know the answer already, or at least the next question to ask, depending on the answer. But if there is nothing they can do about it — if there is no magic pill — some doctors will turn a blind eye.

Dr. Artman agrees, to a point.

"There is some truth to that: If I can't fix it, I don't want to ask," he said. "But it's not that we can't do anything about it. It's that we can't do it alone."

The World Health Organization agrees, and urges expanded psychosocial support in schools and other community settings to help young people with mental illness. Prevention, the WHO says, begins with being aware and understanding early warning signs and symptoms.

There was a time, Dr. Artman pointed out, when society had mostly accepted the dangers and the tragedies of drunken driving. But today, there are designated drivers and other programs, and our perspective has changed.

"We need a movement," he said. "We need a change in society. We need to figure this out."

One of the complicating factors in the discussion about mental health is determining what influences a person's psychological state. In the case of an infectious disease, such as influenza, doctors know there are germs that invade the body. They can be dealt with and the illness goes away. In mental health, it's not so simple.

What is known is that mental health affects other aspects of health. In 2015, the WHO published a study that noted "mental disorders of all kinds are associated with an increased risk of onset of a wide range of chronic physical conditions."

"Good mental health is integral to human health and well-being," it wrote.

Dr. Soden, director of the Division of Development and Behavioral Sciences, said she had seen a lot of progress addressing mental health concerns — inside her hospital and elsewhere — and more on the way. At Children's Mercy, child psychologists are regular members of the medical team in certain specialties, such as cancer. That makes care more efficient, effective and holistic. In San Diego, for instance, Rady Children's Hospital is offering a mental health urgent-care center to make access easier. In Columbus, Ohio, Nationwide Children's Hospital has announced plans for a dedicated half-million-square-foot mental health pavilion to provide treatment and research. Some hospitals are using videoconferencing to provide "telepsychiatry" for patients to reduce travel burdens and increase access to care.

Also at Children's Mercy, the admission process is being revamped and communication with families improved. The hospital has implemented a suicide screening program for pre-teen and teen patients. It has proven successful in getting help to some patients before a crisis.

The Acute Mental Health Screening team provides screening, referral and case management for patients who come into the emergency rooms. The team completed 1,244 assessments in 2017. This work helps streamline treatment for patients with mental health emergencies.

The hospital also addresses mental health through the Social Work department's Child and Family Therapy program. The team provides workshops, consultations and treatments to help families improve relationships and cope with stress and trauma. Nearly 400 patients and families were helped through the program in 2017.

Dr. Soden said the hospital was also working on a mental health smartphone app for children and adolescents with acute mental health concerns. The object of the app would be to improve access and control costs. The project has these goals:

Improved communication between families and mental health providers by tracking symptoms on the smartphone between visits. This could allow for faster feedback or changes in treatment.

Providing the patient instant access to his or her safety plan and information in a format that is easy to read, easy to understand and easy to reach.

Increased understanding of a patient's own emotional, psychological and social well-being. With the proposed app, a patient could monitor his or her illness and immediately find information about it.

The Children's Mercy Center for Pediatric Genomic Medicine and the Clinical Pharmacology program are also playing a part with better diagnostics and pharmaceuticals.

"The medications are getting better," Dr. Soden said. "We are beginning to understand how they affect the genes."

Recognizing that mental health conditions may first be diagnosed by a general pediatrician or family-practice doctor, Children's Mercy has armed its own primary-care offices with the right resources, protocols and tools to care for patients with a broad range of behavioral health needs.

As a result, all five Children's Mercy primary care sites in 2018 received the "Distinction in Behavioral Health Integration" from the National Committee for Quality Assurance. Children's Mercy was the first organization in the country to receive that recognition.

"Adding [mental] health care services in a primary care setting is a real opportunity for patients," said Margaret E. O'Kane, president of the National Committee for Quality Assurance. "It knocks down barriers to behavioral care and improves overall health."

Children's Mercy operates five primary care sites: Beacon Clinic, Children's Mercy West, Teen Primary Care, Operation Breakthrough and Primary Care Clinics on Broadway. They provide care for more than 44,000 infants, children and young adults on both sides of the state line in the Kansas City metro area. Children's Mercy Primary Care employs more than 100 medical providers, including physicians and nurse practitioners, and provides outpatient education for medical residents and medical students.

The work in the Children's Mercy primary care sites is part of a broader strategy to work with doctors across the metro area to care for children with mental health concerns. A recent study found that 77 percent of parents nationwide would first go to their family doctor or pediatrician for help with a child who is experiencing mental health problems. For that to be effective, the pediatricians need to have the resources to help.

In some cases, the primary care doctors should be able to provide initial care that could prevent a greater problem. In most places, however, there is no effective training for doctors on how to evaluate patients for mental health problems. Often the doctor's reaction is to refer the child to a Children's Mercy specialist or an outside child psychologist. That often overwhelmed the mental health care system.

In 2017, Children's Mercy introduced its Mental Health Master Class for primary care doctors. The two-day course teaches the doctors about mental health screening and offers initial treatment options. The goal is to demonstrate how primary care doctors can work with Children's Mercy.

Integrating mental health with primary care is not common, said Kirsten

Weltmer, MD, Medical Director, Patient Centered Medical Home at Children's Mercy. In an attempt to change that, the Master Class provides a foundation in mental health for doctors and guidelines for screening and treatment of depression, anxiety, ADHD and other diagnoses often seen in pediatric and family practice offices.

Patients and nurses: On the sun porch atop the old Children's Mercy building in the late 1940s ...

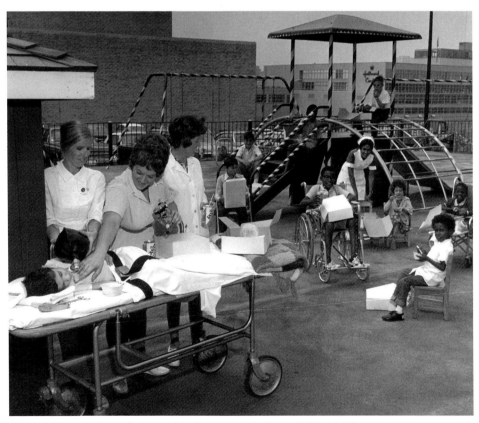

... And at a playground in the 1970s at the latest Children's Mercy campus.

Dr. Mike Artman, chair of pediatrics

Dr. Jay Portnoy, chief of Asthma, Allergy and Immunology.

Parent Care unit

The first chaplain at Children's Mercy, Dane Sommer.

"We can't do it alone anymore": Dr. Daryl Lynch, adolescent medicine.

"It's impossible to ignore the importance of the family": Dr. Brad Warady.

An exclusive interview with Randall O'Donnell, PhD

The most satisfying challenge of Dr. Randall (Rand) O'Donnell's career was developing Arkansas Children's Hospital, where he has acted as COO and CEO for the past 12 years, from a small 87-bed facility to a comprehensive tertiary care provider serving the entire region. Before 1982, children with serious illnesses had to leave the state for care. Dr. O'Donnell helped the hospital reach its goal to care for Arkansas' children at home and make sure every child gets the best care available.

Dr. O'Donnell chose Children's Mercy because Kansas City is closer to family in Des Moines and Omaha for him and for his wife, Melva. Before Little Rock, Dr. O'Donnell was administrator at The Children's Hospital of Buffalo in New York. So the O'Donnells have been far from family for a long time. When Dr. O'Donnell learned more about CMH and saw how committed our board is to helping us grow and serving even more children in the region, he wanted to be part of a hospital that wants to be know as the best.

His first challenges at Children's Mercy will be building rapport with and understanding for all employees and staff; establishing CMH in the political arenas as a national voice on health care reimbursement; helping to see our expansion to completion.

In an ever-changing health care environment, Dr. O'Donnell plans to be FAIR, making sure Children's Mercy is a place where every employee can grow in their field and have a voice, and FLEXIBLE, making sure his calendar isn't booked tight with meetings and appointments that would keep people in the hospital from dropping in to see him or keep him from dropping in to see people in the hospital. He doesn't know how to do a

Dr. O'Donnell's favorite spot in the world is Hong Kong. During vacation there, he saw the country as a gateway to the developing countries of Asia. He believes that in Hong Kong, as in Romania, Americans can do the most good by allowing the people to learn for us. We can show them what it's like to live in a free capitalistic society just by being there, and letting them ask what they want to know.

If Dr. O'Donnell could walk in someone else's shoes for a day, he would pick his wife's, believing that afterward, they'd have a lot more harmony and peace in the family structure and more time for their kids because they'd spend less time working out misunderstandings.

The best book he ever read was the Grapes of Wrath, by John Steinbeck because it really honed his sensitivity to peoples' needs and to tragedies that most of us never face.

The most comfortable clothes Dr. O'Donnell owns are a pair of old Levis, a flannel shirt and Reeboks.

The greatest thing Dr. O'Donnell's parents ever said was, "You can do anything you want with your life."

The most important thing Dr. O'Donnell tries to do for his three children, now 10, 6 and 3, is to let them know, especially his girls, that they can do anything anyone else can and to encourage them to set their sites as high as they want and aim for more than material gain.

The wildest thing Dr. O'Donnell ever did was in college when he climbed a water tower in the middle of the night on a dare (and didn't get caught). Next to that, being a suds-lover in Little Rock is pretty wild.

The most embarrassing thing Dr. O'Donnell ever did was during a high school basketball game. His team had a win in the

Rand O'Donnell as new CEO of Children's Mercy in 1993. His card said the patient was "The Boss" and a screen capture of a hospital video showed Dr. O'Donnell with his "bosses."

Alan Gamis, MD, head of oncology.

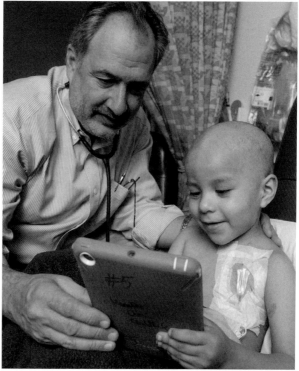

Denise Dowd, MD, became a nurse and then a physician.

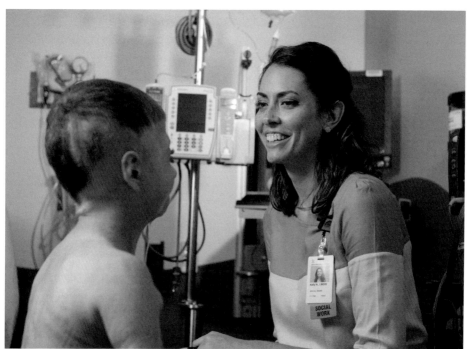

Social worker with patient

CHAPTER 7
....

Meeting children and families in their world

The scene was tense. More tense than normal, even for neonatal intensive care.

The baby — a little boy born at 35 weeks' gestation — was breathing erratically. A nurse next to the incubator looked at the bold lights and numbers on the monitors. She checked the wires and tubes connected to the patient. Something wasn't right. She called for a doctor. Another nurse came over to see what was happening.

The parents, having just returned from a break and a bite to eat, moved in closer, maybe too close.

"What's happening?" they wanted to know. "Is something wrong? Is our baby OK?" Their teenage daughter looked up from her phone and tried to see inside the bed at her baby brother.

More people showed up. The parents looked around quizzically because they didn't recognize most of them or what they were doing. The small room was filling up. Tense seconds, which seemed much longer, passed as caregivers checked the monitors and tubes, listened to his breathing and looked at the little boy.

"That's not right," the doctor finally said. And he quickly began adjusting the feeding tube.

The parents' concern ratcheted up another notch: "How could this happen?"

Their voices grew louder, forcing others to raise their own voices to be heard.

"What does this mean? Who did this to my baby? Do you people even know what you're doing?"

The doctor turned to the father, the most vocal of the family, and tried to reassure him: "We need to get your son stabilized and then we can talk."

That quieted Dad a bit, but he stayed near the doctor, invading his space, right next to the bed where his newborn son struggled to breathe.

A nurse called Child Life to have a specialist come in and help with the big sister, who looked to be in shock. A social worker also entered the room. Someone asked the parents whether they wanted to talk with a Patient Advocate.

The parents still were unsure who all these people were. All they wanted was for their baby to be OK.

Nurses and a doctor went about their work. The Child Life specialist, acting on little information and with no time to assess the family or the situation, put an arm around the sister and led her off to the side, out of the way. She asked whether she wanted to stay or go. They went.

The parents, meanwhile, continued to shout questions at doctors and nurses: "Who can we trust? Who's in charge here? Will our baby be OK?"

The doctor, satisfied the baby was stable, turned to mom and dad, relaxing just a bit. Now they had time to talk. ...

"Cut!" came a voice over a loudspeaker in the ceiling. "Very good. Let's talk about it."

This scene really happened at Children's Mercy, but it wasn't real, and it wasn't in the NICU. It happened in the Simulation Center, where staff members of all kinds undergo training. The three disciplines devoted entirely to psychosocial care — Child Life, Social Work and Chaplaincy — participated to improve their communication, their understanding of other people's roles and their own critical thinking skills in times of crisis. The "parents" were professional actors. Except for them and instructors like Dr. Chris Kennedy, an emergency medicine physician who helps direct the simulation program and plans the exercises, few people knew the scenario in advance.

The outcome of the exercise depended on how the parents and psychosocial staff reacted. Although the incident itself was not real, the learning was.

"This is kind of like the worst nightmare," said the Child Life specialist who participated in the drill. "There's no time for a briefing. You have no information on the family. You just go."

Although it's only practice, there was real tension in the room as parents bombarded doctors with questions and family members cried or lashed out. The small room was filled with people: shouting, questioning or huddling in a corner trying to stay out of the way.

The one word the participants and the psychosocial staff watching through a video feed used to describe the situation: chaos.

This could be any day, or every day, at Children's Mercy.

Child Life in action

The first reaction when most people learn about Child Life is that it's all fun and games. And part of it is, as demonstrated in the playrooms on each of the inpatient floors or by the outside groups that come to the hospital for Wacky Science Wednesday or weekly bingo nights. But it goes much deeper than that.

More than any other staffers in the hospital, the Child Life specialists concentrate on the emotional aspects of care. They help infants, children, youth and families cope with the stress and uncertainty of illness, injury, trauma, disability and loss.

Child Life specialists ask a lot of questions, they listen and they are constantly assessing, doing their best to comfort children who face medical problems. Child Life specialists often are the "safe" person in the room because they don't poke and prod and they don't give shots. If children don't want to do something suggested by Child Life, they don't have to. It's all about providing a sense of normality and control in an abnormal and chaotic situation.

Welcome to the day-to-day world of Child Life.

Each inpatient floor at Children's Mercy has a designated playroom. It's not a room otherwise used for staff meetings, and it's not a storeroom. No medical procedures. No medications. It's used for nothing else.

It's open 24 hours a day for children and their parents. In each playroom, there is a daily designated playtime with a Child Life specialist.

In a playroom one day, an adult looked over the sparkles and glue and paper trashing the table and remarked, "We're making a mess here."

"Ya-a-y-y! This is fun!" shouted a little girl wearing a hospital gown who was tethered to an IV pole. She moved from place to place in the room like a perfectly healthy 3-year-old. She was oblivious to the beep-beep of monitors as she went to work on a snow globe.

On another side of the room, a smaller boy, also connected to a monitor, crawled around on a play mat, seemingly without a care in the world. "Whoa!" he cried as he spied a toy he hadn't seen the day before. "Look at this!"

The little girl's grandmother came to the playroom with a new bag of toys. She talked with the activity coordinator about progress and prognosis. Clearly, there was a relationship between the two. There was confidence. The coordinator, who has a master's degree in social work, offered a smile and some advice.

Grandma listened. Afterward, she said of her little charge: "She just loves it in here. She can be a kid."

The Child Life team has a goal of seeing every child every day. Each morning, the team checks patient logs to see who is visiting. Staffers get to know some of the patients and families because they are frequent visitors or because their inpatient stays are long. Regardless, they try to quickly assess the circumstances, ask lots of questions and determine the best way to help the child and family. They try to spend more time or give special attention to patients with extra trouble coping, higher stress levels or a lack of family support.

On a different floor, another play group was under way. On this occasion, only one little boy had chosen to attend. That's OK with the activity coordinator, who appeared to cherish one-on-one time. The young boy was busy gluing together the little plastic cups in which medication is often delivered. The goal is to make the cups familiar, not something to fear.

While the play went on, so did conversation, sometimes between patients and activity coordinators and other times between children:

"What's your favorite color?" "Do you like to play video games?" "What Avenger do you like the most?"

Sharing a hospital experience creates a special bond between patients. Sometimes they hug. High fives are common. Parents join in play if they want. Some choose the time to take a break. They know their children have someone safe and friendly at their beck and call.

Some hospital floors can be quiet, which is good for some patients but boring and lonely for others. Play groups are an important part of helping children avoid social isolation.

Special activities are also planned to help break up the patients' days and weeks of hospitalization. One of those is the Teddy Bear Clinic, where children get to engage in medical play to help make them comfortable with common hospital procedures.

On this afternoon, a large meeting room was transformed into the Teddy Bear Clinic and all patients interested in and able to make the trip from inpatient units were welcomed. Volunteers helped with those in wheelchairs or sometimes in wagons. Parents could come along for the fun and the distraction.

First, the children received a teddy bear and "admitted" it to the hospital. That required that the bear have a name.

"Let's call him Bubba," a 9-year-old patient said. And then she reconsidered: "Maybe Kayla is better."

At the play blood-pressure station, children saw how cuffs were applied to the bears and how pressure was measured. Next, they learned about X-rays and how they could see inside the body. The radiology technician showed X-rays of dozens of shapes. There were fish and lizards and bones. The "patients" visited the dentist or learned about the various components of blood in their own test tube. Red and white glitter substituted for red and white cells and mineral oil for plasma.

If the "patient" bears needed surgery, the children learned about the different smells — strawberry, banana, orange, bubblegum and root beer — of the anesthesia, or "sleepy air" as it is known at Children's Mercy. (The most popular choice among real-life patients? Bubblegum.)

There was even a music therapist, offering a break to the children as they made their way through the pretend hospital. They sang songs and laughed and watched their cares float away.

The Teddy Bear Clinic happens once a year during Child Life Week; one-on-one education about procedures and tests customized for the specific children goes on year-round. The clinic is one of about 70 special events annually at Children's Mercy designed to help children relax and have a little fun. Other special events include regular bingo games and visits by sports figures, other celebrities, and local and Big 12 team mascots, many of whom take time to play games and just hang out with patients.

Another special event is a talent show that transforms the normally serene Lisa Barth Chapel into a lively auditorium of song, dance and chaos. At one of the shows, "talent" might have been a generous way to describe the acts, but quality was not on the minds of the crowd that packed the chapel that day. One of the chaplains sang an oddball version of "Old McDonald" and professional soccer players from Sporting KC offered a song and dance. All the performances were received with cheers and bright eyes and laughs. They erased everyone's cares for at least a little while.

Evening events form another part of the special programming. Pet Pals brings specially trained dogs to the hospital each week with their owners. Partners in Play involves groups of volunteers who come in several times a year to engage the children in a variety of activities. One group, from the Harley Davidson factory in Kansas City, has visited for years. A weekly bingo game also gets children out of their rooms — not just for a game, but for the social activity.

Pet Pals is not the only time patients have the chance to interact with a dog. Children's Mercy also employs two "facility dogs," Hope and Hunter.

At Children's Mercy Hospital Kansas, Hope and her primary handler, Allison Bowring, make the rounds to as many patients as possible. Some patients don't like dogs or don't want them around, which is fine. Others would spend all day with them if they could.

In one room, with the patient's consent, Hope jumped up on the bed and settled in on a blanket that Bowring brought to minimize the mess of dog hair. What happened next was almost magical: Hope practically disappeared. The patient, a

13-year-old with an eating disorder, began petting the dog and talking with Allison. The sense of calm in the room was palpable. There was a wide-ranging conversation about dogs, about boys, about TV, about life.

Even when there are games going on, it's not just for fun. Consider this scenario:

One time, nurses on an inpatient unit thought it would be a good idea to make visiting the playroom a bonus for a patient doing his physical therapy. The Child Life specialist thought otherwise: play is too important for children. It should not be used as a reward. It's their way of learning, of coping, or processing. Instead, the specialist came up with a game to use as incentive. She knew the patient was a huge Avengers movie fan, so she laminated six Avengers characters and posted them around the inpatient floor. The game was designed so the young patient had to leave his room to find all the characters. There would be a prize when he found all six. At first, he had trouble getting out of bed. But he wanted to find those Avengers! By the end of the day, he was wheeling around the floor on his tricycle, yelling excitedly when he found one, then two and finally all six of the superheroes.

Who says therapy has to be a drag?

Games can be an important distraction as well as a way to form a connection between child and adult so they can talk about important matters. Child Life specialists and activity coordinators ask a lot of questions and engage in a lot of conversation. They are processing, assessing and relaying that information to the care team. One place this is most obvious and important is in the clinic for children who have been abused.

Consider the case of a 4-year-old girl who was brought in for a sexual assault exam. The child showed no outward sign of trauma. With mom out of the room talking with a social worker and nurse, the Child Life specialist introduced herself to the little girl and told her she was there to play for a little while before her exam. The girl's brown eyes lit up: a new playmate! The specialist took a seat in a close-to-the-floor chair, put hands on her knees and smiled. "What do you want to play?"

The patient moved around the clinic waiting room, touching all the toys before settling on a kitchen baking set. She talked non-stop. Bright and bubbly, you'd never have known anything had happened to her. But it had. As she talked, and as the Child Life specialist asked questions, details of her home life became clear.

Mom was "sad at her." The girl kept saying if her new playmate, the Child Life specialist, wasn't good she was going to call the police. Police are not your friend, she told the specialist: "They're going to come and shoot you."

Mom reappeared and remained with her daughter while the staff members retreated to confer. Mom denied any kind of domestic violence and said she was unsure what could have happened to her daughter. But the girl had become withdrawn and begun wetting the bed. She believed everything was her fault. The staff shared theories and thoughts in their preparation for the exam.

The Child Life specialist returned to the waiting room. Her new little friend was excited and shouted, "Do you want to dance?" But it was not the time for dancing. Now, it was time to get ready for the doctor to take a look at her.

"Let me show you," the specialist said while holding a doll.

Step by step, she explained how the exam would go, listening to the doll's heart, shining a light in her eyes, showing off her "hospital pajamas." The girl was hardly interested. She kept picking up the pretend phone to call the police. She was all over the place, physically and verbally.

All that meant something to the trained child development staff. They were assessing, analyzing and preparing.

The little girl's appointment was going to be a long one, which is not unusual. In many cases, it's impossible to know how long some exams, conversations or therapeutic play sessions will last. No two cases are the same.

The Emergency Room, for instance, is by definition a place of uncertainty. One minute can be quiet and the next chaotic. Child Life in the ER often focuses more on siblings than on the patients, depending on the situation. As in the example from the Simulation Center, Child Life staffers often find themselves comforting, playing with or otherwise distracting brothers and sisters while parents, doctors and nurses tend to emergency patients.

Child Life is called whenever a trauma victim comes into the Emergency Room, but immediate medical needs are the primary concern of the trauma team.

"We're still trying to find our place in the trauma room," one Child Life Specialist said. That often means taking parents or siblings to the side — away from the hubbub — and offering a warm touch or a listening ear. Things move fast in the Emergency Room. A lot of people are involved in care and sometimes parents "get lost" or are in shock themselves. Child Life helps explain what is going on. As in everything they do, Child Life staffers' role is to provide comfort and a sense of normality in an abnormal situation.

Still another kind of Child Life intervention happens in the Neonatal Intensive Care Unit. There, tiny babies need care that's completely different from that of the 4-year-old in the child abuse clinic. Among the advanced and intimidating machinery and soft lights, parents may need a heavy helping of assistance, too. Their babies are fragile and their skin may be practically see-through, and parents may not feel comfortable even touching them. But touch is important for bonding and comforting the tiny ones. Because many parents are unable to stay at the hospital around the clock — they have jobs or other children to care for — Child

Life or nursing may leave notes about developmental milestones. Sometimes, parents miss seeing their baby lifting his or her head for the first time and gazing up at the brand-new world. The notes keep them updated.

On the surface, Child Life specialists seem to have a sweet job. They play peek-a-boo with babies or make different facial expressions — all part of "developmental play." Some parents come by this naturally, but others need to be shown. New parents are often overwhelmed, as well as exhausted, and need role models. Child Life explains how the babies are developing and describes their emotional needs. They often create journals for parents, provide them lists of questions to ask and milestones to watch for. They help decorate NICU rooms to provide visual or aural stimulation.

Brothers and sisters of the newborns also have distinctive needs. Because they often are unable to visit, they're encouraged to keep in touch with cards and letters. Parents differ on their approach to involving older siblings. Some don't want to share anything to avoid traumatizing them; others understand it's better for the children to have the information. Child Life can provide help in a way children can understand and process, depending on their age.

Another key role for the Child Life specialist is helping children before and during procedures or tests.

A 7-year-old girl recently diagnosed with cancer came into the Infusion Clinic to have an IV inserted for her treatment. Both her parents were with her and nervousness, maybe fear, filled the room. The Child Life specialist began to explain the process and showed the girl one of the "bendy straws" that would be inserted under her skin. The patient touched it and a look of surprise rolled across her bright face. "It doesn't look like it will hurt," she said, looking at mom for reassurance.

Before the tube would be inserted, the nurse would numb the girl's arm. The numbing medicine comes in a sealed contraption. When it's pushed onto the skin, it releases a gas that sounds like the opening of a soda pop can. The nurse offered a test run and the sound — psssssssstttt! — made everyone in the room smile and laugh. The tension slipped out of the room, too, and it was time to proceed.

Distraction therapy is a big part of the job and the girl decided watching one of her favorite cartoons on an iPad would be a good way to avoid watching what the medical team was doing. It worked. With just a little wince by the patient, the job was done, the tube was inserted and the girl and her family left for the day. Treatment would begin the next day and the Child Life specialist would be there again to help explain everything, step by step.

One of the landmark initiatives in the use of distraction involves having Child Life come into the radiology suites and help children during MRIs and CT scans.

These tests require children to lie very still. Once, it was routine to rely on artificial sedation to make that possible. But when Child Life began to work with the children, explaining the procedure before and then remaining with them during the test, the need for sedation dropped significantly. During the scan, patients can watch television, their own videotapes or listen to compact discs. Child Life specialists can provide a comforting presence, hold a hand or sing a song. Reducing the use of sedation creates fewer risks, takes less time, costs less and increases patient and family satisfaction — a win-win-win situation.

Although Child Life staffers know a lot about medical procedures, medicine and therapy, their real value is their understanding of children. They know how to talk with young patients, tailored to age and level of development. They understand that concepts such as illness, or even death, have different meanings for children of different ages or from different cultures. They understand the power of words and their definitions. They know about family dynamics and how they can affect health and healing. They can quickly assess a situation and establish rapport to partner with families to meet the needs of the patients.

And sometimes they know the best thing they can do is to simply hang out and provide a sense of calm.

Music Therapy and Art Therapy are other programs that provide psychosocial care. At Children's Mercy, both are designed to help children cope, relax, socialize and achieve. Children who take part in both programs smile and laugh, despite being in the hospital.

Decades of scientific research have shown how harmful being in the hospital can be for children, emotionally and behaviorally. Child Life is always looking for new ways to help reduce the stress and increase the positivity of hospitalization. Child Life specialists are there to give children a voice and help them cope with uncertainty, loss of control, fear and more.

Social workers cover the gamut

Perhaps more than anyone else at Children's Mercy, social workers have to be ready for anything – *anything* – when they walk into a room and meet a family for the first time. To an extent, that's true for other professionals who tend to the children. But because the scope of social workers' practice is so broad — everything culturally and socially inside and outside the hospital — flexibility is the key to performing their jobs.

When social workers introduce themselves, the tension can almost be felt. The looks on the faces of families and patients are telling: "Who are you? Why are you here?"

Social workers don't dress like doctors or nurses. They usually carry notebooks, not stethoscopes or toys. And because there is a prejudice against social workers, immediately after a social worker gives her name and title, it's often quickly followed up with, "I work for the hospital, not for the state."

"Not for the state" is code for "I'm not here to take your kids away."

Many parents equate social workers with removing abused or endangered children from their homes. That's not the role of the social workers at Children's Mercy. They are, however, mandatory reporters, meaning if they suspect child abuse they are required by law to report it to child welfare authorities. The same is true of nurses, doctors and many other Children's Mercy employees.

Nobody comes to the hospital or medical clinic to see a social worker. But most people see one before they go. Trained to work in a clinical environment and licensed to practice, social workers are especially helpful addressing complexities in families' lives. They recognize individual challenges and special strengths. They develop treatment plans and help the patients and families use their strengths and the resources available to them.

The primary goal of the social workers, under the guidelines of the National Association of Social Workers, is to "help people in need and address social problems." It's broad and it might be overwhelming, but the social workers at Children's Mercy cite one huge motivator: the indomitable spirit of the children they serve.

Relationships are the key to success. In many cases, social workers have the advantage of spending lots of time with the patients or families, getting to know them, their situations and their needs. That is a great help. In other cases — such as Emergency Room visits — trust needs to be established quickly and relationships may be relatively short-lived.

Take, for instance, a summer Sunday afternoon in 2018. A longtime social worker was called to the Emergency Room with the trauma team for a near drowning at a local hotel swimming pool. Within minutes of the call, family members began to arrive, first one carload and then another.

The victim, a 12-year-old boy, was transferred to the Pediatric Intensive Care Unit in critical condition. He had been under water for about five minutes before he was pulled out. Family members continued to come in, filling both sides of the PICU waiting room. Some sat quietly and stared blankly into space. Others wailed while being comforted by extended family members. Still others chatted beneath the ceiling-mounted TV, seemingly as if they were at a family reunion.

On the other side of the locked doors of the PICU, the medical team worked frantically. The weekend social worker did her best to keep up with it all. Providing emotional support was her initial role. She put her arm around one woman. She sat down and leaned in, quietly asking questions, trying to find out what needs — aside from a full recovery by the young boy — the family might have.

"We walk beside them," was how she put it in a moment of reflection. "If they need space, we give them space.

"I see the sacred. I see sadness. I see heroics. Accidents happen. Disease happens." She paused, and thought.

"I sometimes see pure evil, too. That gets to me. But I can't let it show."

She aimed to provide a sense of calm amid the storm that had become their lives. Preventing sadness and shock was not an option, but support without smothering was. The social worker herself had lost two of her own children so she knew exactly the feelings this family was confronting.

One of the boy's grandfathers was looking for someone to blame. His calm demeanor masked the anger that simmered in the words he spoke. The social worker reminded herself that "anger is the mask that fear and sadness wear."

A police detective arrived to collect some facts and the social worker took him into a quiet room where some of the family gathered. She left them alone and went to check in with the nurses so she could update the rest of the family. Back in the waiting room, mom had arrived and wanted desperately to go see her son. A nurse volunteered to take the mom back to the PICU. The social worker introduced them and stayed behind to offer whatever other assistance she could.

It was a whirlwind of medical information, of grief and of juggling the wants and needs of many different people.

And that was just one case on the social worker's plate that afternoon. There were at least two teenage patients who had been admitted and were awaiting transfer to an inpatient psychiatric hospital. Although they were safe at Children's Mercy, the goal was to find them a place to go.

Social workers realize that every family they see has had some kind of crisis. They know they are often seeing families on their worst days. They try not to take anything personally. They can't afford to.

Families have a myriad of needs and most of those needs existed before the medical situation that landed them at Children's Mercy. Those needs may benefit from the expertise of Child Life specialists or chaplains. Along with social workers, these groups provide the bulk of psychosocial support and they often work as a tag team. They also work to support one another so they can remain strong for families.

Social workers in the Emergency Department or who just work weekends don't get to spend a lot of time with families. Similar to ER doctors or nurses, who may prefer briefer encounters with patients, these social workers see only a snapshot of their patients and families.

On the other end of the spectrum is the Children's Mercy Beacon Clinic, where children with medically complex lives come for care. These children may see as many as 15 different specialists and have as many as 200 appointments a year. One of the big roles of the social workers in these cases is helping parents juggle all those appointments while also tending to the needs of their other children and themselves. It's hard for some of these parents to hold down jobs and the pressure on the parents sometimes leads to less-than-peaceful home lives. In the midst of all of this, the medical needs of the patients sometimes take a back seat.

Social workers sometimes must face the delicate balance of medical versus social needs. If a doctor prescribes a certain treatment, but it puts such a burden on the family that it can't follow through, it doesn't have the desired outcome. Social workers help the medical team understand family situations to better coordinate care and make it successful.

Just as in other clinics, social workers in the Beacon Clinic often are initially viewed with skepticism. When they ask questions such as, "What are your hopes and dreams for your child?" some moms and dads are offended. The goal is to have parents think beyond the day-to-day crises of their lives. The questions are designed to help them and their children find joy in their lives.

Once the social workers earn the trust of families — often by showing them how they can help with such things as transportation, securing Medicaid payments or finding a day care center that takes special-needs children so mom can get back to work — they become allies and advocates and develop a close relationship. Many families distrust hospitals and government agencies. They may not want to share much about themselves, their home life, and their social situation. Social Workers work to convince them they are there to help and that, by letting the social workers assist their family, the health of their child could improve, or at least be better managed.

Gaining the trust of families is especially important in the Pediatric Care Center. There, many patients and families struggle with "social determinants of health," such as adequate housing, nutrition and transportation. Poverty is a reality for many of these families and social workers need to understand the family's challenges in order to best help them.

Social workers and others on the medical team employ a variety of screening techniques. They help identify needs; the hard part is finding ways to meet those needs. Social workers say it is becoming harder and harder to help with rent and utilities. Needs are outstripping funding.

Of particular complexity is helping Spanish-speaking families. There are, of course, language and cultural barriers. But in recent years, these have been complicated by vitriolic rhetoric aimed at immigrants and threats of deportation of undocumented residents.

Social workers formed a special task force to determine how they could help these families and how they could earn their trust. The goal, as always, was to provide the best health care for the children. As one social worker put it, if a mom or dad is worried about where they are going to live or where they can be safe, they're not going to worry about making their daughter's six-month well-child visit.

As patients get older, they encounter new health concerns and social workers find themselves in different roles. At the Children's Mercy Teen Clinic, patients come in suffering from depression or thoughts of suicide. Some young women are pregnant. Sexual health is a challenge for many adolescents. Stress is a major health concern, as peer pressure mounts and expectations of performance in school and at jobs add to the burden of growing up, sometimes in unsafe neighborhoods.

The teen clinic offers the very definition of "holistic care."

Adolescence is the age when many patients don't want their parents involved. Sometimes social workers and psychologists work hand-in-hand, one talking with the patient and the other with parents. They compare notes and do their best to come up with a plan to help both the teen and the family.

A lot of work in the Teen Clinic deals with mental health. The staff there says it's good that more attention is being paid to mental health these days, but there are still limited resources and limited knowledge about the best ways to treat these conditions.

"We're better than we used to be," one social worker said. "But we still have a long way to go."

Meeting the medical needs of many of these older patients is often easier than the psychosocial care. For instance, complicated family dynamics and lifestyle adjustments take place as part of the kidney dialysis and transplant program. For many children, and by extension their families, the medical condition defines their lifestyle. Children on kidney dialysis often spend several hours a day, several days a week, hooked up to a machine that cleans their blood. Trips to the hospital and hours in recliners become a major part of life.

Then, if patients are lucky enough to have a transplant, more changes are required. Transplants often happen when patients are older and are expected to take more responsibility for their care. Yet teen patients often do a poor job of adhering to an anti-rejection drug regimen and other lifestyle changes required in their post-transplant lives.

All this complicates the lives of children and their families. Here is where social workers find themselves. They ask lots of questions about diet, about water intake, about energy levels, taking medication, lifestyle, living conditions, work and school.

One teen patient, who was preparing to start college in a few months, admitted to being overwhelmed by the responsibility of taking all her medications on schedule.

"I think I'll get the hang of it," she told the social worker, who emphasized how important it was and asked what kind of support she had at home.

Her mom, she said, was willing to help, but couldn't read the English instructions on the medication. The social worker said she could fix that and offered to call and talk with mom the next day. Dad did not speak or understand English at all, so he sat stoically in the exam room while the social workers and the patient talked. When an interpreter arrived, Dad brightened up. Having the interpreter often relaxes parents and patients, giving them more confidence to ask questions and get answers.

Dad said he didn't understand why his daughter was having trouble following directions "for her own good" and he believed she was old enough to take care of herself. He was pleasant and smiled, but also shook his head "no" as the social worker tried to explain the complexity of the life as a teenage transplant recipient on the cusp of leaving home for college.

"You can't do everything at once," the social worker said.

Dad smiled and told the interpreter he understood. But his daughter said she wasn't so sure and would talk to mom about that, too.

Children with cystic fibrosis present additional social challenges because theirs is a life-long condition. Each week, the medical team — doctor, psychologist, nurse, respiratory therapist, nutritionist, pharmacist and social worker — meet to go over each of the patients coming in for their appointments. Because there is no cure for cystic fibrosis, the team gets to know its patients and families well, so a special bond is formed.

In the meetings, team members discuss the family's needs and decide what's most important to help them. Sometimes, it's most important to talk about medication, so the pharmacist takes the lead. Other times, problems with transportation, housing or school are paramount. For those patients, the social workers lead the appointments.

Few families have the support they need to take care of patients at home so they must come to the hospital for treatment. If a lung transplant is a possibility for the patients, they must commit to moving to St. Louis — the closest lung transplant program — for a minimum of six months, causing a major disruption in their lives.

Social workers often find themselves in the middle of this juggling act.

There's a lot of negotiating with parents and adolescents. There are a lot of hard conversations. There is much hand-holding, and tears and frustrations and anger.

One of the newer programs at Children's Mercy that requires an entire team of experts is Rehabilitation for Amplified Pain Syndrome or RAPS. Rheumatologists, nurses, physical and occupational therapists, music and art therapists, psychologists and social workers come together to treat multiple aspects of the pain.

One of the few of its kind in the country, RAPS helps children in constant pain, where the patients themselves say their nerves are "drama queens," "pain nerves stuck on 10" or are "always in fight-or-flight mode."

Because pain is something that can't be "seen," it is often misunderstood, ignored or denied. In the RAPS program, patients spend hours learning to "trick" their brains into accepting the pain so it's not debilitating. Social workers help them know how to discuss their condition and their treatment with their classmates, many of whom think "it's all in our heads."

The Home Ventilator program is another treatment option that forces a major change in a family's way of life. In it, babies — some born as many as 16 weeks early — are sent home with a ventilator to help them breathe until their bodies develop. The process takes about two years. The babies need almost constant monitoring and often are unable to make sounds because of a tracheotomy tube. Parents miss hearing their babies "coo" or speak.

Social workers try to help families find private home nursing and other resources. They also help with juggling a variety of responsibilities such as jobs, other children and marriages.

"Parents want to take their children home," a social worker said. "Of course, they do. But it's life-changing. It can be overwhelming. There is no way it can't be. I've sat in on hundreds of care conferences and I still get overwhelmed. Families look to us for reassurance for everything. We can't do it all, but we have to try.

"It may sound cliché, but you think you've seen it all and then we're always seeing something new."

Chaplains walk with patients through their journey

If social workers get a look of discomfort from parents when they enter a hospital room and need to explain they're not from the state, imagine the emotions that are stirred when chaplains walk in and introduce themselves.

People instantly think about dying.

"Sometimes, in the midst of a crisis, I don't even tell people I am a chaplain," said Janie Wood, who joined Children's Mercy in 1992. "They don't need to know that right then. I'll just ask how I can help them."

Neither Wood nor any of the other chaplains has anything to hide, it's simply that too many people think a chaplain's only role is to help during dying and grieving.

"We're really here to support people in any way we can," Wood said. "I tell families: I am here to walk your journey with you."

Although perhaps not a traditional part of medicine, Sommer says at Children's Mercy at least the chaplains are firmly rooted as part of the medical team.

"We bring healing to everyone we meet along the way, whether it's a young person or a parent or a grandparent," he said. "Go back to the origins of English words and the word 'healing' is connected to both health and wholeness. Chaplains here bring wholeness and health, in some way, to everyone we meet."

Like other Children's Mercy staff members, chaplains are not meeting families on their best days. Usually, something terrible has happened before chaplains enter the picture — a trauma of some kind or a frightening diagnosis. Doctors and nurses can offer medical treatment, but chaplains are charged with spiritual healing, helping patients and families with questions of "Why" or "Why me?" The answers are often difficult to answer or troubling to accept.

Time and again Sommer, the hospital's first full-time chaplain and leader of the Spiritual Services department since 1987, has seen families confronted with "that unfairness or injustice that is there when a child who is sick or a child is permanently harmed or injured, or a child is facing death."

Despite religious background or tradition, he said, almost all people in those situations find themselves questioning, wondering and looking beyond themselves for answers to difficult questions.

"I know we are all connected by a sense of spirit, a sense of spirituality," Sommer said. "The word 'spirit' itself is connected to the clinical word 'respiration.' It's the same thing: the spirit is that part of us that has to do with our breathing and our living. Our spirituality is what gives us a sense of meaning."

The role of Spiritual Services, therefore, is to help comfort people, to be a non-anxious presence that helps quiet or calm a child or family, and to walk with the families through their journey.

The essence of the chaplain's role is to help parents through difficult times. They are doing a job only special people would do.

"A lot of what we see here," explained Chaplain Seth Sonneville, who joined the hospital in 2014, "are things no parent should have to deal with, no child should have to face.

"So we are here to walk with families through whatever it is they are facing that day, without judgment, so they can make the best decisions."

Sometimes, families disagree with the medical team and the treatments their children are getting. Chaplains sometimes act as go-betweens, impartial observers, remaining above the fray. Chaplains observe what is and is not being said. They stand in the middle of the tension so parents and siblings and other family members are not alone.

Chaplains don't choose sides, but they offer comfort and honor the family in difficult and profound moments that leave even the strongest parents or children questioning their purpose, their lives and the meaning of it all.

"Some people may never agree with the medical team," Sonneville said. "One of the things I learned in training is you can't take people where they're not ready to go."

Among the challenges that chaplains face is understanding the vast array of religious traditions. Helping evangelical Christians waiting for a miracle can be much different from helping a Jehovah's Witness.

"What we need to do is to enable them to talk about what their faith means in the midst of the challenges," Sommer said.

It is the diversity of the families served at Children's Mercy and the hospital's founding principle of being non-sectarian that caused the Lisa Barth Chapel to be declared a place "where all are welcome" when it opened in 2013. The chapel includes a variety of religious articles, a library, a prayer wall, an outdoor garden and a room designed for a hospital bed where families can spend quiet time in end-of-life situations.

Chaplain Becky Crouse, who works primarily in the Neonatal Intensive Care Unit, said the new chapel had opened a variety of possibilities for families who were grieving and, perhaps, preparing for a death. Children who may never get to leave the hospital have a chance to go to the garden just outside the chapel. Families have shared meals in the chapel and invited family and friends to say goodbye to their children.

Sometimes, families or patients don't want the help of chaplains at all. And for the chaplains that's fine.

"The magic is when they invite us in," said Crouse, who joined Children's Mercy in 2003.

Wood recalled one family who dismissed her overtures because the dad had some Bible college experience and the family thought they "had it." After a few unexpected twists and turns in their child's condition, they sought out her counsel.

"Before long, they began to ask me to pray with them," Wood said. "Dad realized there was more to this than he was prepared for. They began to share more openly what they were going through and they knew we had some experience with that."

A mom with a baby in the Pediatric Intensive Care Unit provided another example of the value of chaplains. After being born in the Fetal Health Center the baby, with multiple complications, was transferred first to the Neonatal Intensive Care unit and then to the PICU. The baby was not expected to live much longer.

Despite the baby's difficulties and the terrible options the family faced, doctors and nurses tried to comfort mom, assuring her she was "doing great." But one night it was apparent she wasn't. Alone in the glass-doored room of the PICU, mom cradled the baby, who was connected to machines that whirred and beeped. She rocked back and forth, holding the sick, fragile baby tighter and tighter.

When Sonneville approached, mom didn't want anything to do with him, or anybody else. But he entered the room, quietly sliding open the doors and dropping to his knees in front of the rocking chair. Mom refused to look at him.

Calling on his military background, the quiet-mannered chaplain looked at Mom and said, "I heard you've had a [really bad] day."

Mom looked up and then directly at Sonneville. Her eyes opened wide. She hugged the baby even tighter. And then she unleashed.

She cursed God. She cussed about the medical staff. She was tired of people telling her how well she was doing. She was sick of it. She was angry. She rocked back and forth, back and forth. Sonneville listened. He affirmed her truth. He let her vent "before she lost herself."

As much as she hadn't wanted Sonneville in the room, she appreciated his presence and knew she was not alone. She was relieved that it was OK to be human and to know there was help for her as she prepared to let her baby go. She could take the next step because there was someone walking with her.

In the Gender Pathway Services clinic, a teenage boy wasn't interested in seeing the chaplain either. He was anxious to get on with his transition out of Children's Mercy to a doctor for adults.

But Sonneville decided to visit anyway, just to say hello. What followed was an encounter that can only be described as "spiritual."

After an awkward introduction and handshake, the chaplain sat on a stool and smiled.

"I just wanted to check and see how you're doing," he said. Immediately, a calm presence enveloped the room. There was no tension. No sense of judgment. The fidgeting young man uncrossed his arms and was still. And he began to talk. Not about religion and not about God. But how he wanted to move on with his life. He wanted to leave behind his old self. Were there support groups that could help? Am I OK?

"That was a sacred moment," the chaplain said. "We didn't need to talk about

God. That was sacred language. That was a human moment."

"I don't want to hide anymore."

The young man, 19, had what seemed like a simple concern. Summer was coming and people were beginning to wear shorts and sandals. He sat in the exam room with long jeans, tennis shoes and a bulky sweatshirt.

"I don't want to wear sweatshirts in the summer," he said to the Children's Mercy team checking in with him as they prepared to help him find an adult health care specialist.

So what was the problem?

Well, underneath the sweatshirt and the jeans was the body of a girl. He was in the process of transitioning his physical gender, but hadn't had any surgery. His mom sat nearby, looking at her son, worried as he processed so much stress.

"I don't want to hide anymore. I want to make new friends and I want them to know *me*," he said.

He was saying all this in the GPS Clinic at Children's Mercy. Gender Pathway Services provides family-centered services for transgender, gender-variant and gender-questioning children. As with the other programs at Children's Mercy, the goal at GPS is to support patients' physical, mental and social health and also to support their families as they process gender identity and navigate what the medical field can do for them.

The specialists recognize that each patient has a different "pathway," so they provide care that is unique to each patient and family. The goal is to keep families informed about treatment options and to provide them medical and emotional support.

The team with the young man — a psychologist, nurse and social worker — listened closely and reassured him that they were there to help. They asked questions about his support system and suggested talk-therapy groups he could consider — although none in his hometown and none where he worked. He wanted to keep some things private.

He said he felt depressed sometimes, but he stopped cutting himself five years ago when he began to transition, so things are better. He has trouble making friends and worries, "I feel like I'm nothing." On the other hand, work is going well and he's in line for a promotion.

Emotionally, he was on a roller coaster and it was obvious to everyone — including himself —that he needed all the support he could get.

His journey had been long, but he saw a way out of the morass.

He was thankful for a safe place to go and talk. He acknowledged the support at Children's Mercy.

Yet he was anxious, foot tapping on the floor nonstop. He really wanted surgery. He was ready for more change.

Whether the topic is gender transitioning, cancer treatment or neonatal complications, spiritual services is an important part of whole-child and family treatment.

"If you don't deal with the searching, with the yearning, with the questioning, it impacts many other aspects of your life," Sommer said. "It affects your decision-making. It affects your relationships."

Perhaps the greatest sense of questioning and searching for answers happens when a child dies. As much as Children's Mercy is a place of healing, the reality is that deaths do occur — about 150 a year, or one every two to three days.

"Each case is different," Sommer said. "It never gets easy."

Crouse acknowledges that she gets emotionally involved with her patients and families. She wouldn't want it any other way.

"The day I stop crying is the day I quit," she said.

Crouse remembers as if it were yesterday one little girl who was a patient her entire life, until she died in heart surgery a few days before her first birthday. Naturally, the family was devastated. Their little girl seemed so full of life and love. The chaplain, too, was also heartbroken. On the morning of what would have been the little girl's birthday, Crouse looked out her kitchen window at home and on her deck was a pink balloon with a butterfly design that had floated in by chance. Butterflies are used in the hospital — and elsewhere — as symbols of hope, life and the resurrection.

"I knew right then," Crouse said, "that the little veil between heaven and earth had opened up and this balloon fell out." She collected the balloon and gave it to the family, which had it framed.

About one-third of the deaths at Children's Mercy occur in the Neonatal Intensive Care Unit, where the tiniest, most fragile premature babies go. Because each family and each child are different, dying and its after-effects vary greatly. Chaplains call the NICU the roller coaster: "You can be doing well and then you can crash." Sometimes, families need several days to make decisions necessary to let their child die peacefully. In this time, chaplains and others on the care team collaborate closely to help families.

Dying and death, Sommer said, can be like a Jackson Pollack painting, with many layers, at first glance out of control and senseless. Chaplains, he said, help families through the chaos. At this particularly hard time, Sommer said, the team approach to psychosocial care was essential. Nurses can provide some of the medical knowledge if that helps families, as well as a near-constant presence. Child Life can help siblings understand and cope. Chaplains are a "non-anxious" source of comfort, "open and affirming of all people." He said the team provides multiple perspectives for the family and, maybe most important provides "more hearts to love them."

When death comes

The care provided by Children's Mercy does not end when the child dies. Instead, that's when the hospital's Aftercare Program kicks in.

Wood, along with nurse Chris Casey, started the Aftercare Program in 1996 to provide education, direction, consultation and support for families and staff. As experts in bereavement and grief counseling, the program helps families with emotional healing after the death of a child.

The Aftercare Program provides:

- Sibling grief bags, comfort items and resources to help siblings begin to cope with the death of a brother or sister. Materials are based on the sibling's developmental state and include suggestions for parents on how to speak with children about death and dying.
- Support groups.
- Memory items, including a memory book to which staff members add notes about the children, hand and foot prints, clippings of hair and plaster molds of hands and feet.
- An opportunity to make a square for a memorial quilt that is displayed at the hospital for five years and then stored in the Lisa Barth Chapel.
- End-of-life photography by a professional photographer, and an opportunity to have a professional sketch made from a photograph.
- Personalized follow-up.

Families are surveyed after a year has passed since the child's death, and feedback to the program has been positive. Nurses and chaplains received the highest scores for being available to the parents when they needed them.

"I really appreciate the personal notes in the first year and the quilt," one mom wrote. "I'm so glad you continued to send me information and didn't just drop me because finally, five years later, I am ready and happy to be completing my quilt square."

One of the visible aspects of Aftercare is the annual memorial service, begun in 1997.

"We had no idea how many people would come," Wood said. "But we have some families who continue to come since the very first one."

Typically, about 750 people fill a ballroom in a hotel near the hospital for the service. It includes family speakers on the bereavement journey, prayers, a doctor reading a litany of remembrance, an activity for siblings to do in memory of their brother or sister and an opportunity to write messages to children who have died. The celebration climaxes when everyone moves outdoors and about 300 butterflies are released. The creatures inevitably land on people's shoulders before taking flight up the hill from the hotel toward the hospital.

Crouse said the memorial service helped families affirm that their child had not been forgotten and that his or her life had meaning. In many cases, few people outside the hospital had a chance to know these children, so it is nurses, doctors, chaplains and others who can let families know the spirits of their children live on.

Like the rest of psychosocial care, the work of Aftercare is not merely sentimental. It is essential to the good health of the families and the community.

"If people do not grieve, it affects their health," Wood says. "People will become ill mentally and physically."

Research at Harvard Medical School has found that stress brought on by grief can lead to a variety of physical and emotional issues such as depression, trouble sleeping, feelings of anger and bitterness, anxiety, loss of appetite and general aches and pain.

The death of a loved one — especially a child — can shake the foundation of one's existence. Some grief may resolve itself without help, but in most cases families need support. And unless friends or neighbors have experienced a similar loss, the help needs to come from outside their normal support system.

"When a child dies, the death destroys the dreams and hopes of the parents," Wood said. "Many parents describe the pain that follows as the most intense they have ever experienced and wonder if they will ever be able to feel that life has meaning again.

"The literature says that grief is a normal and natural reaction to loss of any kind. It is a physical, emotional, spiritual and psychological response. Although it is a universal experience, no two people grieve the same, even in the same family."

Quoting bereavement specialist Darcie D. Sims, she said: "Grief is the price we pay for love."

She summed up the importance of the work she and others in the Aftercare Program offered:

"Patient- and family-centered care has always been a part of who we are, and this is why this program exists. The care at Children's Mercy does not stop at the end of life."

On the front lines

Nurses, doctors, housekeepers, security guards, volunteers.

What do they have in common? They all take care of children and families at Children's Mercy. And they all work together to meet the needs of the whole child.

The role of doctors in medicine is obvious and their role in psychosocial care is growing, but nurses are on the front lines of all aspects of patient care. Nurses, many with 12-hour shifts, spend more time at a patient's bedside than any other professionals. The nursing staff at Children's Mercy numbers nearly 3,000, and they care for children and their families around the clock. When parents are away, nurses often stand in for them. They form bonds with patients and families that extend well beyond the inpatient units or the outpatient clinics.

Cheri Hunt, RN, MHA, senior vice president and chief nursing officer for Children's Mercy, has seen great progress in the care for children in her three decades as a nurse at Children's Mercy. The one constant, she said, has been the nurses.

"We are trained to coordinate care among all the different patient care disciplines," she said. "Nurses pull it all together."

As with other health care professionals, not all nurses have the same personality traits or the same skills. But all seem to bring their patients an underlying compassion and commitment to caring. Some nurses, too, seem to have a special touch.

"It's a gift," Hunt said. "The nurses who do it well, who connect effortlessly — it's a gift."

Each May, during Nurses Week, some of those gifts are on display at the annual nursing scholarship ceremony. For a couple of hours, parents, philanthropists and peers take the stage to tell stories about what makes nurses special.

At the 2018 breakfast ceremony, Dee Lyons, a long-time hospital supporter and one of the first to endow a nursing scholarship, recalled for the packed hotel ballroom that, in the early 1990s, the ceremony took place in the hospital's old dark-wood paneled boardroom. There were just a few hundred dollars in scholarships for continuing education to award.

"Well, look around you," she told the ballroom audience. "Look at all of this. Something really great has happened." She then awarded the first of $129,000 in scholarships that would be presented that morning.

Because they perform medical procedures and also give psychosocial support, nurses are in a unique position with families. Often, they act as liaisons between doctors and families, families and Child Life specialists or social workers and doctors.

At the 2018 scholarship ceremony, members of the Children's Relief Association, which operates the Children's Mercy gift shops and donates proceeds to the hospital, said nurses often came to the shops to buy balloons or other treats for patients or their siblings. Their "caring and nurturing spirit" was on full display, they said.

Dale Hensley, who presented a scholarship for nurses in the Pediatric Intensive Care Unit, thanked the nurses who helped care for his daughter.

"We are blessed to have you fighting for our kids," he said. "You give fearlessly and you never forget that at the other end of the chart is a child and a family." Although his daughter did not survive, Hensley said, she lives on "through the light in your eyes and the love in your heart."

"Thank you for connecting at the level of the heart."

Other parents agreed. One said that the way nurses connected with parents and families was the most important and most personal touchstone of their care.

Nurses often make trips to the hospital on their days off or before or after their shifts to see patients who are no longer officially assigned to them. That connection, parents said, helps their children's recovery — and their own. The connection sometimes lasts for years. Nurses, as well as some doctors, are often guests at milestone events such as graduations, weddings and baby showers.

That nurses become a "part of the family" is not a surprise or an accident. In fact, the very basis of providing the best care for children is to do it within the context of the family. When a child is hospitalized, the whole family is affected.

Nurses find themselves juggling the demands and needs of doctors and other care providers with the psychosocial needs of children and parents and families. Sometimes the nurses simply notice when parents need a break. One Christmas, nurse Megan McGurn noticed a mom who was exhausted and struggling to help care for her daughter, a patient. McGurn assured the mom it would be OK if she stepped away; McGurn would take care of her baby and mom could get some rest.

"I awoke the next morning," the mom wrote in a note of thanks, "feeling like I could handle life again. ... This all occurred on Christmas Day, when I couldn't be home with all of my beautiful children, and our nurse had to be at work and away from her family as well. ... She saved my sanity. I was so tired, so lost, so sad and anxious, and she came in like an angel and brought back my humanity. ... I now feel equipped to get through the rest of this illness with my sweet girl."

Another nurse puts his special artistic skills to work to make a difference. Richard McComas, RN, is an operating room nurse who draws cartoons or designs over the chest incision dressing for post-operative heart surgery patients.

"When our kids come back, parents are often appropriately distressed and concerned," one of his co-workers said. "I've noticed when kids come back with his artwork it eases parents' discomfort. Instead of seeing a big scary bandage on their child's chest, they see fun, cute and absolutely amazing artwork that seems to instantly relieve their stress."

The artwork is drawn individually for each child. One little girl, McComas found out, was a fan of the movie "Frozen," so he drew the character Olaf to be placed on her chest.

"When the little girl saw one of her favorite characters on her chest," the co-worker said, "she reached up to touch the dressing and smiled."

Everyone's job

When Children's Mercy was invited in 2006 by the Robert Wood Johnson Foundation to tell others the secret to its culture, one of the keys the authors reported in the hospital's response was to "view all employees as essential contributors to success, rather than as commodities."

Just as parents have been accepted as part of care teams, employees from a variety of jobs not directly involved in patient care also play a role in creating a positive, child- and family-focused environment.

Employees responsible for keeping floors clean or lights working are often overlooked as care providers, but the environment is an important part of healing. Artwork, paint colors, carpeting and design features — all figure into care at Children's Mercy.

Important in creating all-hands-on-deck camaraderie is encouraging communication among employees from all walks of the hospital workforce.

"We don't just walk the walk," said Lonnie Breaux, former director of facilities, in the report to the Robert Wood Johnson Foundation. "We actually talk to each other and seek out input."

The team spirit that permeates the organization began to take root as a result of a complaint. Certain nursing units reported that they could never find a housekeeper when they needed one. Breaux suggested the housekeepers join their teams for their daily direction.

The result has been a feeling of inclusion and pride that can't be simply decreed. Growing mutual respect was even more evident when Howard Thomas was named Employee of the Year in 2005. His job? Keeping clean the 32 elevators across the hospital campus.

"After they step out of their car in the parking garage," Breaux said of patients and visitors, "one of Howard's elevators is their first contact with the hospital. Making that first impression a good one is essential."

Security officers form another part of the first impression. All adult visitors, including family members, are required to pass through security screening. They must present photo identification and are asked where they're headed or who they want to see. In such a brief encounter forming a relationship with families can be difficult

At the security stations on any given morning, moms and dads are often juggling children or food or balloons — sometimes all of them — and then are asked to search their wallets for an ID. The security guards show immense patience and frequently get to know some of the regular visitors by sight, if not by name.

"Give me five!" one of the officers said to a young boy in a wagon as his mom waited to be checked in. "You back again? You're looking good today! Hope you have a great one." The boy and his mom pushed through, down the hallway toward the surgery clinic, smiles on faces, chatting about the nice man who welcomed them back.

"If I can make them feel a little better, that's the job," the officer said afterward. "We're here for them."

The philosophy that patient care is everyone's job is integrated into everything from new employee orientation to internal communications campaigns. In fact, in 2018, a series of posters and computer messages to employees emphasized the role all employees had in the recognition of Children's Mercy as one of the best children's hospitals in the country by *U.S. News and World Report.*

"I Take Shots, Not Give Them," declared the headline of a poster featuring one of the hospital's photographers. "But I helped earn this [award.]"

Other similar messages were from people who work in Government Relations, Information Technology and Philanthropy.

"I work with charitable donors, not blood donors," the poster said. "But I helped earn this."

Done out of love

More than 1,500 volunteers help out at Children's Mercy, everywhere from the emergency room and outpatient clinics to the gift and snack shops.

They help during play time and special events. They help families find their way through the maze of hallways and buildings. Sometimes, they rock babies. They are essential to the psychosocial care of children and families.

Volunteer Lois Lakey, otherwise known as Grandma Lois, has held a coveted volunteer position at Children's Mercy for two decades. For 20 to 30 hours every week, Grandma Lois can be found sitting in a chair in the Neonatal Intensive Care Unit with a critically ill newborn in her lap.

When families cannot be at their baby's bedside night and day, Lois comes in, offering comfort, support and a lullaby or two.

Although Grandma Lois focuses mostly on caring for babies, she's made a marked difference in the lives of people across the hospital, including parents. Sometimes she brings clothes to the hospital for families.

"I try to be the best I can be with these babies," she said, "but, it's not only with the babies I try to share. The parents, they need love too."

By late 2018, Grandma Lois, who was turning 83, had amassed a staggering 26,000 volunteer hours. When she first became a volunteer, she was led around the hospital to see what spots were available.

"We came to the NICU and a baby was crying and the nurse was busy," Lois said. "This is the spot."

Countless babies have been held and comforted by Grandma Lois over the years. She said she loved every one of them. Sometimes she receives pictures and updates of former NICU patients.

If she could share one piece of advice with every baby, Grandma Lois said she would tell them: "I love you. Be the best thing you can be in this world."

Rewarding nurses' compassion

Children's Mercy is one of about 1,000 hospitals in the United States that participates in the DAISY Award for Extraordinary Nurses. The national program, begun in 1999 by the family of J. Patrick Barnes in California to thank nurses such as those who cared for Patrick, recognizes nurses not just for their clinical skills, but particularly for the compassion they show patients and families day in and day out. According to the foundation that sponsors the awards, DAISY stands for Diseases Attacking the Immune System.

Nurses are nominated by nurse administrators, peers, doctors, patients and families. Children's Mercy presents DAISY awards to about six nurses each year for a variety of good works. Examples culled from hundreds of nominations include:

- "During an inpatient stay for our daughter, Katie [Heide], RN, exemplified what it means to be a pediatric nurse at Children's Mercy. She treated our daughter with respect and kindness, but did so while recognizing our daughter's maturity and incorporated her into some of the decision-making about her care. She was a tremendous advocate for our daughter."

- Luz Galeano, RN, received 12 nominations one month from her peers and physicians. She was commended for "making me feel welcome in the department," for her "nurturing support of our patients" and because she "handles difficult situations with great calm and does everything with a smile." Her co-workers said she got to know patients personally, went well beyond addressing their immediate medical needs and was a "gift" for the children.

- Several people — including co-workers and patient family members — told stories about Holly Godshall, RN, and a little girl who did not survive. "The nurse that worked with my niece and my sister is an angel on earth. She was so incredibly sweet and comforting to my sister. ... Then she came to my niece's Celebration of Life service. When she came and my sister saw her, my sister went to her and just wept in her loving arms. She just held my sister and let her weep. ... Words cannot express the gratitude I have for this sweet, caring, compassionate lady."

- Katie Fee, RN, BSN, goes out of her way — on her day off and on different patient floors — to keep in touch with her patients. "Katie became so much more than a nurse," one mom wrote. "She became someone we trusted and talked to. She became a friend."

- Marcy Page, RN, BSN, takes a keen interest in her patients, including one boy who was a long-term patient. The day after he expressed his love of pistachios, Marcy brought in the ingredients to make a salad with pistachios and showed him how to make it. "This is not an unusual thing for Marcy to do. This small gesture made a huge impact on this patient's long-term stay."

- A mom nominated Shea Scanlon, RN, BSN, for the DAISY award, but also took time to recognize others on the staff. "The hospital can be a scary place in general. ... The first few hours after [our son] was admitted were a blur of words and procedures I didn't understand. ... Then our night nurse came on, and is the sole reason we made it through the night without losing our minds. ... I was hoping to never see the inside of your hospital, especially the ICU, but I cannot tell you how thankful I am to have Shea as our nurse to make it easier on all of us. Although our son was sick, we had a wonderful experience at Children's Mercy with everyone we encountered, from the security guards to the cafeteria staff and most certainly all of our nurses. ... We are blessed to have this hospital in our city."

....

CHAPTER 8

The future is bright.
The future is here.

One thing about Children's Mercy: it stops at very little when it comes to taking care of kids. Every bit of them — mind, body and spirit.

Psychosocial care, the care that offers a warm, comforting embrace to the children who need help, means looking after all those things that affect children: their emotions, developmental stages, homes, communities, environment and extended families.

The attention health care providers pay to children's lives outside the walls of the hospital has increased. Imagine for a minute that children are like goldfish swimming in a bowl. When they get sick, it's not enough to look only at the fish. We need to look at the water, too.

The challenge is daunting. There is new science and now there are new threats. The future depends on succeeding with children who won't be children forever. The eventual goal is healthy adults and a healthy community.

Health care beyond illness

The biggest challenge Children's Mercy and others face may be providing care for all the various influences on a child's health. Social factors, such as where and how a child lives, can be far more important to good health than genetic makeup and the work of health care professionals.

"When it comes to overall health, ZIP code is more important than genetic code," the Blue Cross Blue Shield Institute said in its 2017 annual report. "ZIP codes represent the access or lack of access to important resources, such as primary care physicians, pharmacies, fitness centers and nutritional food options. The infrastructure of a ZIP code determines the underlying behavior patterns observed in communities across America."

According to some estimates, as much as 60 percent of good health is driven by social determinants, including lifestyle, poverty and environment. Thirty percent is determined by genetics — you're born with it — and the remaining 10 percent comes from access to and the quality and quantity of health care. Based on those percentages, the medical community must help address the broad, psychosocial needs of patients, not just the medical needs.

One way Children's Mercy does this is through the hospital's Council for Violence Prevention, formed in 2010. The council is addressing self-directed violence, including suicide; intimate partner violence; bullying; human trafficking, and psychological trauma. Two hundred Children's Mercy employees are directly involved in these efforts. Indirectly, through screening programs designed to determine risks of suicide or domestic violence, hundreds more take part.

To reduce violence and help children and families, members of the council recognize that they must collaborate with police, food pantries, day-care centers, schools, churches and other groups outside Children's Mercy. And the hospital has a long history of working with the community.

The Internal Revenue Service requires nonprofit hospitals to report their "community benefit," but it does not define exactly how they are supposed to show that. The IRS does identify broad categories of work necessary to justify tax-exempt status for hospitals. The work must improve access to health care, enhance the health of the community, advance medical or health knowledge or relieve or reduce the burden of government or other community efforts. Details are left to individual hospitals.

From July 1, 2016, to June 30, 2017, Children's Mercy calculated $195 million in community benefit. The bulk of that, $115 million, was for care for which it received little or no reimbursement. The rest included the cost of medical education, research and community health programs and partnerships.

The hospital uses its Community Health Needs Assessment to help it decide where to allocate resources. The assessment, done every three years at the direction of the IRS, includes extensive data collection and interviews with a wide variety of care partners and patient families. In addition, the assessment includes a plan to address needs.

The IRS gives little definitive direction of what to address and how. The government leaves those answers up to individual nonprofit hospitals, based on their own communities.

But how far should a hospital go? If part of what is making children and adults sick involves lifestyle or behavior choices, should that be the hospital's responsibility? Is it the doctor's job to make sure that his patients get proper nutrition outside the hospital? Should the nurse's job include worrying about the safety of playgrounds at city parks? For more and more hospitals and health professionals, the answer to all these is "Yes."

Hospitals across the country are responding in different ways. Ohio is full of examples:

- The children's hospitals in Akron and Dayton take direct aim at the opioid crisis.
- The company that owns Toledo Children's Hospital opened a small, full-service grocery, where shoppers can also get help with job training, wellness, financial education and more.
- Cincinnati Children's developed a program, copied around the country, to help parents nurture their children, especially during the first crucial 1,000 days of life.
- Nationwide Children's in Columbus has helped revitalize a residential neighborhood next door to the hospital to ensure that at least some of its patients have safe, clean and accessible places to live.

Not far away, in Chicago, extraordinary efforts are underway at one children's hospital and a variety of agencies to stem violence, obesity, drug and alcohol abuse and poor mental health.

Far from traditional medicine, these efforts show a trend and commitment to whole-child care.

"This is a new generation," said Karen Sheehan, MD, emergency room and preventive medicine doctor at Lurie Children's Hospital in Chicago, who has been active in community outreach programs for 30 years. "There is growing social activism and growing physician activism. A lot of the junior faculty are really jazzed about what we're doing. Even some of the older faculty want to do more."

At the Children's Hospital Association, which tracks industry trends and activities, this sort of community activism has been difficult for some to embrace, particularly hospital leaders who "like to stay in their lanes," said Karen Hill, director of Community and Child Health at CHA.

"A lot of CEOs don't like to take chances," she said. "It's hard to predict success in some of this community work."

Some of Children's Mercy partners see the hospital as the proverbial 800-pound gorilla because of its extraordinary growth throughout the city and its favored status among elite philanthropists.

Indeed, size and scope can have advantages, yet smaller community agencies remain essential "boots on the ground" that can recognize specific needs. Neighborhood associations and faith-based groups also may have access to grants and other resources that are out of reach for Children's Mercy.

As part of its partnering work, Children's Mercy organized and hosted the city's first Child Health Summit after completion of the 2016 Community Health Needs Assessment. The summit drew more than 150 people, representing dozens of organizations throughout Kansas City. At the end of a long day, the group voted that the No. 1 issue threatening the health of children and the entire community was poverty — daunting, insidious and multi-faceted.

Rather than being overwhelmed, Children's Mercy and other partners began to break off pieces of the larger threats to good health and develop plans to address them.

Among the new efforts at Children's Mercy are a summer lunch program that feeds hundreds of children each week at the hospital cafeteria. Also being developed is a transportation-on-demand program for families who need help getting to doctor appointments.

Children's Mercy also provides small grants to community agencies. In one case, a non-profit that provides beds for those in need faced devastation after a flood destroyed its warehouse and inventory. Children's Mercy was able to provide a small amount of money to keep the agency alive.

Center for Community Connections

A major new initiative to help families is the Children's Mercy Center for Community Connections, opened in January 2017 on the seventh floor of the Children's Mercy Clinics on Broadway building. The goal of the center is guiding families through not only the Children's Mercy system, but also through a vast array of other resources.

"This space says to the families, 'You are important; let us help you,'" said Dr. Jeff Colvin, medical director of the center.

One of the most important efforts of the center is a partnership with Kansas Legal Services, which has operated in some form at Children's Mercy since 2007. Lawyers help families on both sides of the state line with a variety of legal issues, including guardianship, child custody, housing, family law, Social Security income appeals and denials of public benefits. Over the years, more than 3,000 families have been helped.

In the nine months ending in March 2018, nearly 300 families were referred from other parts of Children's Mercy to the Center for Community Connections. Almost 40 percent were referred for housing problems. Other top concerns were nutrition, utilities, transportation and employment.

"There has been a slow evolution in health care to understand what's important to health," Dr. Colvin said. "It's not just the traditional things. But it is social determinants, mental health, unintentional injury.

"Some patients' social needs are overwhelming to a point that they interfere with access to care and adherence to treatment. It's difficult for a family to follow a treatment plan when they're worried about where they're going to sleep that night."

The center's services are in addition to the help of social workers who see patients and families in the various medical clinics. If a family's needs are complex or specialized — legal, for instance — social workers refer people to the center. Some staff members spend days combing through resources to help families get help, whether it's a job, car repairs or educational opportunities. There are two full-time social workers who are part of the center team.

"It's not always easy," said Debby Brookstein, senior director of Social Work. "It's like running a marathon and it's filled with landmines."

The center offers the federal nutrition supplement program Women, Infants and Children to those who qualify, as well as a variety of injury prevention items such as car seats and bicycle helmets. Patient financial services are available as well as social work family therapists. For many families, the center is a true one-stop shop.

The center operates more than a mile away from the larger, hectic main hospital campus, Brookstein said, to convey a sense of peace and calm:

"Many of our families are here in a state of chaos, so we wanted them to know this was a safe place."

Collaboration at Operation Breakthrough

For two decades, another important partner for the hospital has been Kansas City's largest Early Head Start program and social service center, Operation Breakthrough.

The program operates in the urban core, where half of all children under 6 live in homes with incomes under the poverty line, which was $25,100 for a family of four in 2018.

Children's Mercy operates a medical clinic at Operation Breakthrough and provides social workers to help families. It also provides mental health services with psychologists, psychiatrists and developmental pediatricians.

In a report about the Operation Breakthrough work, Dr. Cox, the hospital's former chief operating officer, and David Westbrook, its senior vice president for strategy and innovation, explained the commitment:

"Children are the conscience of a community. The care and attention a community gives each individual child becomes the most elegant measure of that community's regard for itself. Yet, by most meaningful measures, there is not much elegance associated with society's regard for the nation's children."

The two were writing in *Current Problems in Pediatric and Adolescent Health Care* in its September 2017 issue. That month, the entire journal was devoted to the Children's Mercy/Operation Breakthrough collaboration to deal with toxic stress and adverse childhood experiences. It detailed how the relationship began in 1998 and how it had grown, stumbled, changed and survived.

"The partnership with Operation Breakthrough represents a new kind of relationship," Dr. Cox and Westbrook wrote. "Hospitals, in partnership with community organizations, government and the private sector are moving away from services solely based on interventions when people are sick. Instead, we are trying to create and stimulate the development of resources aimed at promoting children's good health and then helping these children stay healthy.

"We can make life better for these children, but not if we wait until a crisis brings them to the hospital."

Children's Mercy is always looking for new and innovative ways to meet the needs of its patients and their families. Its Center for Pediatric Innovation is, at its core, a place for employees to brainstorm ideas and turn them into services.

"Ideas come from every corner of the hospital — from physicians and nurses to human resources and security," said Krista Nelson, director of innovation development. "It's a great example of how empowered we all should feel to generate and advance creative solutions."

Examples of recent initiatives to tend to psychosocial needs include:

- **Rhythm of the Heart:** The Music Therapy team records a child's heartbeat and then uses it as the beat and tempo of a custom-written melody that serves as a personalized memento of the time at Children's Mercy. Depending on family preference, it could be a country, rock or pop song. Older patients can write their own songs.

- **Staying in for Prom:** For most high school students, going to the prom is a landmark event in their personal lives. But what if you can't go out because you're stuck in the hospital? Children's Mercy transformed one of its rooms into a magical ballroom and some teen patients dressed up and invited dates for a special night. Members of Sporting KC, the professional soccer team, attended as dance partners, sending some of the patients "over the moon" for prom. The next year, the hospital took this idea further by putting on an in-house "summer camp" for chronically ill patients to have experiences to tell their classmates when they returned to school.

- **Medicine, Research and the Arts:** When a Children's Mercy researcher was confronted with explaining complicated medical procedures and terms to patient families — especially those who did not understand English – she turned to an unusual partner: the Kansas City Art Institute. Upperclassmen take the concepts of drawing blood or performing endoscopies and turn them into visuals with easy-to-understand information sheets. The project was funded in part by the National Endowment for the Arts and is now, after four years, expanding to include other departments beyond medical research at Children's Mercy. The hospital is now working with the sculpture department about creating 3-D models of hearts and bones.

- **Walking on Life Support.** After a 16-year-old patient had been on life support for months, she wanted to get up and walk around, believing it would speed her recovery. There was no protocol for patients on ECMO (extracorporeal membrane oxygenation) to walk; they needed to be tethered to the machine that was keeping them alive. But the teenager was persistent, her mom was encouraging and the doctors were willing to try new things and shake up procedures. With all of them working together, the young lady managed to walk the halls, visit the chapel and get a manicure, surprising and inspiring many.

- **Tackling financial concerns up front.** Despite the hospital's 120-plus-year commitment never to turn away a child because of an inability to pay, the cost of health care is a big concern for many families. To ease some of that worry, a Financial Clearance Team has been developed to merge the skills and work of Children's Mercy pre-registration, pre-certification, financial counseling and patient financial services teams. The idea is to give families more information about costs, insurance and assistance up front. "The aim … is to engage families early on to address financial concerns, so that by the time of the visit, their focus can remain on the clinical care of their child," said Amy Crawford, director of Patient Access.

Social workers go to school

Perhaps the boldest of the new initiatives is a partnership begun in 2017 with the Blue Valley School District in suburban Kansas City. Twenty social workers were assigned to the schools in the 2017-18 school year.

"Kids today face more pressures and stress than ever before," said Carey Spain, a director of Social Work. "It takes a village to support them through the challenging times. These social workers are a vital link between the student/family and the school, home and community."

This continues a long history Children's Mercy has had with the public schools. For more than a century a school has operated inside Children's Mercy. For decades

Children's Mercy has hosted a health conference for school nurses.

In the Blue Valley partnership, social workers join school counselors and psychologists to provide individual services and instruction for small and large groups. Mark Schmidt, Blue Valley's assistant superintendent for well-being and student services, said the program did so well in its first year that more social workers were added for the next year so no social worker had more than two schools to cover.

Since the Great Recession of 2007 to 2009, he said, the relatively affluent Blue Valley district has seen an increase in its numbers of homeless children and children on free- or reduced-price lunches. At the same time, parents, students and educators have called attention to higher stress because of school and community pressures.

"If we're not taking care of the everyday needs of the children, we're just spinning our wheels (in the classrooms)," Schmidt said.

One of the more troubling issues is teen suicide. In the 2016-17 school year, the district identified and took steps to help 300 students at medium or high risk of being depressed or suicidal.

"I wish we had the answers," Schmidt said. "Social media gets some of the blame. We are a school district of high achievers and with that comes high expectations. And there is not enough mental health support in the community."

Preliminary data from the social work experiment are promising. The social workers met with more than 2,000 students. Nearly 80 percent of the referrals were for behavior matters, anxiety and other mental health needs. Suspensions in elementary schools dropped 30 percent from the previous three years.

The Children's Mercy social workers, Schmidt said, "have helped students with self-regulation, connected homeless families with community resources, smoothed the transition for children in foster care, prevented student suicide and collaborated with our existing school counselors and school psychologists.

"In a very short time, the social workers have become a critical part of our mental health support team."

The patient experience

One of the growing fields of interest in the health care industry is "patient experience," which includes psychosocial and family-centered practices. One of the leading advocates of the movement is the Beryl Institute, based in Texas. The institute defines patient experience as the sum of all interactions between a patient and an organization.

Patient experience is shifting from being physician-centered to family-centered.

It's a tall order, but it can be summed up this way: Treat other people with respect, listen to them, consider their perspective and communicate with them.

In the chaotic and sometimes frightening atmosphere of the hospital, it can be easy to forget how to treat people well, experts say. Medicine may need a checklist for patient experience, not just for surgery or other medical treatments, said Dr. Anna Reisman, writing in an internet blog popular among physicians. Her checklist:

- Treat a patient like a family member, with dignity and respect
- Be gentle and honest
- Don't rush
- Make them comfortable
- Acknowledge their fear
- Don't sit behind a desk
- Encourage questions
- Grade yourself on how you feel when you leave the room. If you leave with a smile, give yourself an A.

"To be sure, it may be distressing for patients to think that hospital staff need such reminders," Dr. Reisman wrote. "But the whole point of checklists is to ensure that we don't overlook the most obvious tasks. ... I propose we acknowledge that a bad patient experience is a medical error."

Dr. Atul Gawande, a surgeon and best-selling author of *The Checklist Manifesto* among other books, uses two words to frame this matter: patient vs. person. As much as health care professionals talk about patient-centered care, the patient experience is still one that happens *to* you, not *with* you. The goal should be to help people have a human experience, he writes, not a patient experience.

Organizations with better patient experiences also have better safety records and better financial margins, according to Thomas H. Lee, MD, chief medical officer at the patient experience consulting firm Press Ganey Associates. Lee and his colleagues looked at various safety measures — readmissions, hospital-acquired conditions, adverse safety events (when patients are harmed unintentionally) — and compared them to data on patient experience and satisfaction.

"For every comparison," Dr. Lee wrote in 2017, "the clinical quality performance was better in the hospitals with the better patient experience performance.

"There is good news for chief financial officers, too. ... Financial margins for the hospitals in the top quartile of patients' likelihood to recommend (a standard patient satisfaction measure), were 4.8 percent higher than those in the bottom quartile."

Children's Mercy, in an effort to more closely align patient satisfaction and hospital performance, moved responsibility for patient and family surveys to the Department of Quality Improvement and Patient Safety. The department developed "Family Experience Tracers" that collect information, comments and data from families throughout their stays in the hospital.

Lee Woodruff, whose husband Bob was an ABC News anchor when he suffered a traumatic brain injury while covering the war in Iraq in 2006, spoke at Beryl's Patient Experience 2018 national conference in Chicago.

Communication and compassion, she said, make all the difference in the world for families.

"Words matter," Woodruff said. "And that takes no time, costs no money. Your words can vastly change the outcome for the family."

For Woodruff, and so many other families, it's not just about medicine. Doctors gave Bob Woodruff little chance of recovery and he spent months in the hospital. Lee had a basic question when Bob was lying in a coma and it had nothing to do with medicine: "Would he still love me when he wakes up?"

As of 2018, he was back reporting for ABC on special assignments. And the answer to her question: Yes!

"Please, keep the door open for hope," she said. "There is always hope. If I want to believe in a miracle, what does it cost you?"

Children's hospitals in the lead

The patient experience movement shows that adult hospitals are catching on to the value of psychosocial care. With children's hospitals leading the way, evidence mounts that psychosocial and family-centered care improve health outcomes.

In 2010, the U.S. Congress authorized the independent, nonprofit Patient-Centered Outcomes Research Institute. It is designed to provide evidence to help patients, caregivers, insurance companies, employers and public policy makers make well-informed decisions on health.

"Patients are our true north," according to the Institute website.

Advocates of patient-centered care, including those at children's hospitals, point to evidence of improved outcomes. According to The Advisory Board, a national health care consulting and research firm:

- Patient-centered care is associated with decreased use and lower costs.
- Higher patient satisfaction — which stems from better communication and care coordination — brings improved compliance with care recommendations and lower inpatient mortality rates.

- Higher patient satisfaction with inpatient care and discharge planning is associated with lower 30-day readmission rates

The Patient-Centered Outcomes Research Institute helps fund research on patient-centered topics, and Children's Mercy has received some funding from it. Among the topics studied are what outcomes matter most to children and parents, as opposed to those regarded as important by the medical team; why patients and families rate some hospital experiences better than others, and how to help doctors and patients communicate better to improve care.

As a result of this and other work, more providers are seeing that psychosocial care is a crucial component of health care.

U.S. News & World Report, whose annual rankings of the best children's hospitals are closely watched in the industry, has changed its survey over the years to include psychosocial measures.

When it started ranking children's hospitals, *U.S. News* did so based strictly on reputation. It surveyed pediatric specialists across the country and asked them simply, "Where is the best care for kids?" But in recent years questions about psychosocial care have increased. In 2017 those measures accounted for 3.3 percent to 4.2 percent of the total score, depending on the specialty. The lowest was in cardiology and the highest in neurology.

In the *U.S. News* survey, questions are asked about access to Child Life and family support specialists, psychologists, in-person interpreters, schools, sleep areas for parents and siblings, a Ronald McDonald House and family resource center. The survey also quizzes hospitals about the role of families in advisory committees or treatment.

Dr. Warady, Children's Mercy Hospital's chief of nephrology, serves on one of the physician advisory committees to *U.S. News*. He said there was no watershed moment that pushed psychosocial care into the consideration of what makes a children's hospital "best."

"But we all recognize it's important," he said of his peers on the advisory committee.

In much of medicine, children's hospitals have followed the lead of adult institutions. After all, the adult health care world is much larger and has many more resources devoted to it.

As Dr. O'Donnell, the former Children's Mercy CEO, has pointed out, he disappointed some of his graduate school advisors when he chose to "limit" himself by choosing pediatrics. But there are areas where children's hospitals lead and adult hospitals follow, such as patient experience. Among those areas, according to a summer 2017 article in *Children's Hospitals Today,* the magazine of the Children's Hospital Association:

- Family-centered care, including patient and family involvement, education and formal parent roles in advisory capacities.
- Patient safety, in part because children's hospitals were first to throw aside competition and work together to improve the quality of care.
- Facility design and the healing environment. "Children's hospitals are known for their distinctive environments," the magazine said, "which include right-sized equipment, distraction therapy ... and more. This helps young patients feel safe, more comfortable and less scared. Adult institutions are starting to see that kids aren't the only ones who benefit from this type of healing environment."
- Care coordination and collaboration, in recognition of the complex nature of the health of many patients. The Children's Health Association is working with 10 of its members, including Children's Mercy, on a $23 million grant from the Center for Medicare and Medicaid Innovation to improve coordination of resources for children with complex medical conditions.

Care coordination, in part, makes sure all the parts of a child's care are working together. With the potential for multiple physicians, nurses, therapists and psychosocial specialists all working to care for children and their families, the chances of duplication and inefficiency are high. That not only complicates care and potentially reduces its effectiveness, but also can drive up costs.

Children's Mercy uses "patient tracers" to follow patients from their initial encounter with the hospital through all the steps back to health. Care coordinators keep track of the many people, programs, buildings, pieces of medical equipment and community resources involved in a patient's care.

This example, which is hypothetical, shows the complex nature of a child's care, with more than a dozen people across several buildings and departments involved. It demonstrates the importance of communication:

Tristan is an 11-year-old with asthma and diabetes. His family has several barriers to his care: mom is single and under-employed and has two younger children to care for.

After an ambulance ride, Tristan arrives in the emergency room. There, a social worker and nurse discuss how Tristan has been to the ER several times already this year for the same ailment — asthma. Once again, Tristan is admitted to the hospital. Then the ER staff transfers his care to a nurse care manager and social worker in the inpatient unit.

The nurse care manager does a "readmission" screening and determines that Tristan can benefit from home care to help manage his medications and also to educate the family about diabetes.

While Tristan is in the hospital, he visits a play room and talks with a patient activity coordinator. He is visited by a Child Life specialist and a music therapist. They pass along any pertinent information they uncover about Tristan or his family to Tristan's nurse.

The social workers and nurse care managers at the office of the primary-care doctor receive information about Tristan's most recent hospital stay. They work with Tristan and his mom to help make sure they make it to appointments and are handling care responsibilities at home.

The medical team in the primary care office collaborates with the Pediatric Care Network care team to coordinate care while using benefits through the patient's health insurance.

Because of transportation difficulties, the social worker — now the third social worker helping Tristan — aids Tristan's mom in setting up the KidCare Anywhere computer application so the family can see a doctor from home.

The Home Care nurse helps with medication and the asthma and diabetes care plans and also arranges for a Children's Mercy Environmental Services home assessment program. The assessment shows extensive mold in the home and the social worker speaks with the landlord about dealing with that problem.

The social worker also provides Tristan's mom a letter for her employer so she can be with Tristan while he is in the hospital and can take him to future appointments. The social worker, with the family's permission, also contacts Tristan's school to help with his medical and counseling support. She also works on providing transportation and visits by nutritionists, asthma educators and others.

Care at home is truly family-centered

Home care is one piece of the care puzzle that is quickly changing and growing. More care is being shifted home from hospitals and doctors' offices. In 2017, home-care visits by Children's Mercy staff increased by 21 percent over 2016 to nearly 5,000. That is in addition to more than 10,000 deliveries of formula, supplies, nebulizers, wheelchairs, infusion pumps and more.

Home care is less expensive than hospitalization and usually less stressful and frightening for children. It also personifies the concept of "patient centeredness."

"The home is a much more nurturing environment," said Kellie Wheatley, a physical therapist with Children's Home Care. "Children learn better at home, especially young children."

That opinion was echoed by the mom of a 2-year-old victim of a brain tumor. Wheatley was helping the child learn to walk and sit up after the tumor robbed him of those abilities.

"He's more irritable when he's at the hospital," the mother said. "Here, he's in his own environment. He's happier here. Once he got home, he just blossomed. There's something magical about home."

However, home also presents problems. Most houses weren't built to be turned into intensive-care units or rehab hospitals, and most family members are not nurses or doctors.

"We're asking parents to do extremely complex care in the home environment," said Anita Powell, RN, director of inpatient nurse care management/utilization review. "There are a lot of medical decisions that weigh on the psychosocial. We need to ask all the right questions."

At one home, in an apartment complex in midtown Kansas City, a respiratory therapist, social worker and nurse met for a visit with a baby who was born prematurely and was on a breathing monitor. In a crowded though neat and clean living room, several adults came and went in the course of the mid-morning Home Care visit. Evidence of a recent meal — a pizza box, Coca-Cola and breakfast cereal — were evident in the kitchen and dining room.

Mom listened intently and was able to repeat the instructions from the nurse. She tested the alarm on the monitor. After the TV was turned down, there was discussion of weight gain, day care, employment and living arrangements.

"It's easier to establish a rapport in the home," said Christina Kohl, a respiratory therapist for Children's Home Care. "People are more comfortable in their homes. We can see how they really live."

Home care visitors need to assess situations quickly, ask lots of questions and read between the lines.

"We see things in the home visits that we would never know in the clinic," Kohl said.

Home-care specialists also need to be flexible, even more so than their colleagues who work with patients inside the walls of the hospitals and clinics. Home is a far less controlled environment.

"Every single family we see is different," said Stephanie McDanel, RN, a home care nurse, who was examining a young patient on the floor of an in-home day-care unit where she met the mom during her lunch break. In addition to helping the mom, McDanel visited with the day-care providers so they were aware of the child's condition and needs. In a single hour-long visit, McDanel wore many different caps: educator, therapist and counselor.

"We'll meet at day care or in schools or at home," Kohl said. "This is all about meeting their needs."

Transitioning

As pediatric health care has improved, a new need has emerged among children suffering from chronic conditions: "transitioning" them from care at a children's hospital to care in the adult world.

Life expectancy doubled in the 20th century and infant mortality dropped from 165 in every 1,000 births to seven in every 1,000. More children lived to adulthood, yet chronic conditions of childhood sometimes remained with them.

Most children's hospitals provide a one-stop shop for medical specialties, something fairly uncommon in the adult health care industry. Transitioning helps patients and families make the otherwise abrupt adjustment.

Children's Mercy is recognized as a national leader in transitioning. To begin with, as patients at Children's Mercy mature they take more responsibility for their own care and reduce the responsibility felt by their parents. The goal is to have the patients successfully transferred to an adult provider by age 22.

There are more than 10,000 patients age 18 or older on the books of Children's Mercy.

"We're not there yet, but we're working on it," said Dr. Ann Modrcin. "From the very beginning, we've said, 'We're going to transition all of our eligible patients; they deserve the attention required to make sure they enter the adult health care world with a plan.'"

Studies have shown that if children, especially those with complex needs, do not make the transition successfully their medical costs escalate and complication rates increase. Treatment for deadly conditions may be delayed.

As part of the process, Children's Mercy has published the booklet "All About Me: A guide to taking charge of your health care." The booklet, written for patients by the hospital's Teen Advisory Board, explains the need for making the transition:

"As much as we would like to, we can't be patients at Children's Mercy forever. We are all growing up, getting older, our bodies are changing and some diseases may move into different stages. There comes a time when we have to move on."

Patients and medical teams develop individual plans for each child. Just as with other aspects of care, the transition is not one-size-fits all. The process begins before the teen years, when patients begin to have discussions about taking care of themselves. By 15, they spend part of their doctor visits without parents or guardians in the room. By 18, the goal is for the patient to be fully involved in his or her own care.

In January 2018, Children's Mercy leaders co-wrote an article in the journal *Health and Social Work* about implementing a transition model. The Family and Teen advisory boards, along with nurses, doctors, social workers, care assistants and hospital executives have worked together on the program.

"We're trying to be leaders in ... building the infrastructure to make it as easy as possible to be successful," said Terri Hickman, a social worker and manager of the transition program. "We are eager to share what we've learned."

Is there a limit to what we can do?

There is no denying the commitment of Children's Mercy to the care of children. The hospital continues to expand with new buildings, staff and programs. Leadership is committed to facing the challenges and has declared Children's Mercy will stop at nothing.

"It is a beautiful thing, idealistic, that we're doing in children's hospitals," said Dr. John Lantos, bioethicist at Children's Mercy.

Yet the pressures and trials the hospital faces mount.

Poverty, poor housing, lousy nutrition, declining immunization rates, new, deadly germs and staggering and confounding mental health problems threaten children and their families. High costs and potential cuts in insurance reimbursements endanger hospitals' and families' financial bottom lines.

Is there a point of no return?

Dr. Lantos echoed what Children's Mercy leaders wrote about the necessity of its work with Operation Breakthrough: that the needs of many children are not being met at home or school or in their neighborhoods. There is abundant evidence of social neglect — much as there was more than 100 years ago, when Children's Mercy was founded. When the children end up in the hospital, Dr. Lantos said, that neglect begins to be turned 180 degrees.

"It's over the top, maybe even perverse," he said. "We make sure they have *everything*. But only while they are here. What happens when they leave?"

It's not surprising that the authors of the Transitioning booklet, who were teen patients as members of the Teen Advisory Board, wrote: "*As much as we would like to, we can't be patients at Children's Mercy forever.*"

At Children's Mercy, Dr. Lantos teaches the only pediatric bioethics certification program in the world. In it, students ask many of the same tough questions. During a recent class, students conducted research on such topics as transgender children and the right to transition, refusal of treatment by cancer patients, the deficiency of care for mental illness, the limits of adolescent decision-making and learning from families how to deliver bad news.

One of the former students in his class, Dr. Amy Caruso Brown, assistant professor of pediatrics and bioethics at New York Upstate Medical University, returned to Kansas City in 2018 to give a talk titled: "Is being treated in a children's hospital a right or a privilege?"

For many at Children's Mercy, the answer is both.

When Paul Kempinski joined Children's Mercy in November 2018, taking the helm from Dr. O'Donnell, he found an organization that is, in his words, "evolving to become one of the best pediatric hospitals in the country."

The new president and CEO sees psychosocial care as foundational to the high-qualty care and culture, character and commitment of Children's Mercy.

"We have a 120-year history of pushing forward, breaking through barriers and challenging the status quo," Kempinski said. "Our founders were innovators and disrupters. They recognized that children are not just little adults, and they pioneered psychosocial care before it was even a term."

He is not about to become complacent.

"Believing great is good enough," he said, "is not in our DNA. We recognize there are many challenges facing pediatrics and we will face them. We also recognize that there are many challenges facing our children and their families and we must do all we can to serve and care for them — every bit of them."

Next stop: A trauma-informed institution

When it comes to placing children and families at the center of it all, Children's Mercy and the rest of the health care industry have come a long way. But there is a new goal on the horizon, one that is broad in scope and arduous in its demands.

It pushes all employees to reach beyond the notion of family-centered care to a new, complementary focus: to provide care with the knowledge of the influence that trauma has on the lives of children, their families and all those who take care of them.

The notion of "trauma-informed care" has been around since the 1990s, but only recently has it come into full focus and practice. Acknowledging the impact of trauma has been aided by research that shows the dangers of toxic stress.

In health care, trauma often is thought of in terms of medical trauma such as traffic accidents. "Trauma-informed care" refers to psychological trauma — an experience that overwhelms an individual, family or community's ability to cope. No one is immune from the effects of traumatic stress. It can have lasting adverse effects on mental, physical, emotion and social well-being.

Trauma-informed care requires that hospitals not only be aware of the impact of trauma, but also adopt practices that treat and serve patients without doing more harm.

"Just like universal precautions when around blood; we always wear gloves because we don't want to risk infection," said Patty Davis, a social worker at Children's Mercy who is program manager of Trauma-Informed care. "With trauma-informed care, we need to take similar trauma-sensitive precautions to avoid unintentional harm or re-traumatizing our patients based on their past experiences."

Consider a case in the Children's Mercy emergency room a couple of years ago.

A child was brought in after an asthma attack. Doctors and nurses treated the asthma effectively. The child received medication and an opportunity to rest to make sure the crisis had passed. His mother got instructions on how to care for him at home and was told it was time to go.

But the mother refused. She questioned whether her son was really out of the woods. She was adamant that he was not ready to go home. She was visibly upset and in tears. She refused to leave.

The doctor could not understand. He tried to assure her that her son was OK, that the hospital had done all it could and should. There were other patients in more urgent need. Still, she would not leave.

The physician chalked it up to a "difficult" parent and asked a nurse to help. The nurse, also part of a busy emergency room staff, had similar problems communicating.

Next, a social worker was called. Social workers often are called to help with "difficult" or "non-compliant" families so doctors and nurses can move on to more medically urgent matters. By taking time, asking more questions and asking them with a greater sense of understanding, the social worker discovered that about a year ago, the child's brother died from an asthma complication. Mother was terrified.

That traumatic experience influenced her reactions to the medical recommendations to go home. By not working harder to understand her, the hospital staff was unintentionally causing more emotional reaction and further mistrust of the medical system.

"Had we been more aware, more sensitive, more questioning, we might have avoided this situation," Davis said. "The more we understand that trauma and toxic stress affect everyone who comes in the door, then we change our lens. We become a lot more curious about what has happened, use empathetic listening and further discover what we can do to meet the needs of these children."

In this case, the social worker finally understood mom's concerns and gave her enough information to make her comfortable about going home.

A trauma-informed perspective reinforces the notion that all people want to live their best lives. It reminds us that people thrive when feeling safe. When a person is not, or is otherwise struggling to meet expectations of the health care team, the team could ask itself, What is getting in the way? Is there a barrier to trust? Is there true collaboration and empowering going on? Does this person feel safe enough to share concerns about the medical recommendations?

Part of being sensitive to patients is choosing the best approach. Instead of asking: "What is wrong with you?" a caregiver can ask, "What has happened to you?" The difference is suggesting you want to fix someone as opposed to wanting to understand them. Likewise, instead of thinking, "What's wrong with these people?" you can question, "What has happened to the people in that community?" The approach moves from judgment to offering to be an ally.

"Too often, we have treated the symptoms and not the history," Davis said. "This is an extension of holistic, patient-centered care,"

Research shows that trauma-informed care works to improve health. A 2005 national study found decreases in symptoms of trauma and mental illness and in substance use in hospitals that practiced trauma-informed care. Likewise, studies have shown decreases in children's levels of verbal aggression and making physical threats in the hospital. Truman Medical Center in Kansas City — across the street from Children's Mercy Hospital — saw a 35 percent reduction in assaults on the staff between 2014 and 2016 after embracing trauma-informed care.

It's equally important to acknowledge the impact of trauma on the staff, Davis said.

Being directly exposed to or having knowledge of others' traumatic stressors day in and day out can take its toll. A health care system that addresses only the impact of trauma on patients and families will struggle with secondary traumatic stress, staff burnout and turnover.

Addressing the secondary traumatic stress experienced by staff is not an afterthought, but rather should be the foundation of the trauma-informed health care practice.

Although Children's Mercy Hosptial is on its way — it began its formal program in trauma-informed care in 2014 — there remains a long way to go before it's woven into the fabric of the organization. Davis said the culture change can be expected to take 10 to 20 years.

But having seen how Children's Mercy has embraced psychosocial care, such an evolution does not sound impossible. It's just another part of the journey.

A Child Life staffer, Sydney Shyrock, right, with patients in a playgroup at Children's Mercy.

Social work leaders.

A patient pats Hope, a therapy dog handled by Allison Bowring.

Guitarist and music therapist Ashley Scheufler works with a patient.

At the Children's Mercy Beacon Clinic, a social worker, Amanda Textor, second from the right, talked with a patient's family through an interpreter, Patricia Haynes.

Worship services at the hospital.

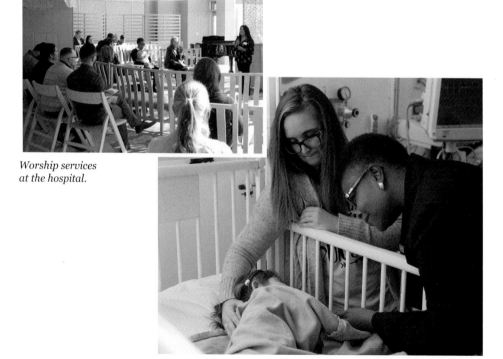

Children's Mercy Chaplain Tracey Woods, right, with a patient in Intensive Care.

Nurses Anna Lynch, above left and Jasma Ellis, above right, and their charges.

Operating-room nurse Richard McComas, who creates on the chests of heart-surgery patients images such as this symbol for Northwest Missouri State University.

Dr. Rupal Gupta at Operation Breakthrough in Kansas City's urban core.

*Where friendliness reigns: Security supervisor Ed Stewart
at Children's Mercy entrance.*

*Volunteer Lois Lacey — "Grandma Lois." For
two decades she has comforted critically ill
newborns.*

*Lacey Lee, one of the social workers assigned to
the Blue Valley School District.*

155

Posters used by Children's Mercy to communicate the importance of every employee.

Rand O'Donnell, backer of psychosocial care, now retired as CEO of Children's Mercy.

Paul Kempinski, new CEO of Children's Mercy.

Designed to heal

Positive outcomes at children's hospitals depend on a variety of things. Talented doctors and nurses are essential. Medical technologies provide opportunities unheard of in the past. Pharmaceuticals hold the key for many patients. And, as this book points out, the many professionals dedicated to psychosocial care bring an extra dimension that provides comfort, facilitates healing and addresses a multitude of health-related concerns.

But what about the hospital and clinic buildings where so much of this happens? Do they play a role? Does the physical environment affect health and well-being?

Without a doubt, yes.

"We know, scientifically, that a comforting environment helps healing," said Dr. Mike Artman, chair of pediatrics at Children's Mercy. "It makes sense."

A sign above the lobby at Children's Mercy Hospital welcomes visitors on behalf of the children to *their* hospital: "Please come in … To be well, to learn, to discover. This place of care, love and hope is for you."

The children's own hospital — it's the idea designers keep in mind.

Donald Ross, an artist called "Scribe" by all who know him, joined Children's Mercy in 2003 as its first in-house artist.

"We try to see things from the perspective of the child," he said. "We want to convey a sense of peace and safety."

Upon walking in the front doors of the Adele Hall Campus, children's art work is on display. It sends an immediate message: We like kids and we're proud of them.

"It's like putting their artwork up on the refrigerator," said Melissa Stover, a Child Life specialist at Children's Mercy since 1997 who works closely with Scribe.

To the uninitiated, Scribe said, it might appear that the art and colors and graphics displayed throughout the hospital are random. But that is hardly the case.

One thing that sets the aesthetic tone of the hospital is color. Proper color use is both an art and a science. Certain colors evoke certain responses and, depending on the part of the building, some colors might not be appropriate. According to Scribe:

- **Pink** is a soothing color. It can be protective and full of compassion.

- **Red** is bold. The color is known to release adrenalin, which elevates blood pressure. It is attention-getting. It is exciting. It is also the color of blood and, for the most part, best avoided in hospitals.

- **Blue** is a calming color. It is infinite and heavenly. It lowers blood pressure and heart beat. It is the color of communication.
- **Yellow** is optimistic. It is warm, inviting, uplifting.
- **Earth** tones are grounding.
- **Orange** is energetic.
- **Black** is authoritative and can evoke a feeling of mystery or emptiness.

In a presentation to the Association of Child Life Professionals in 2018, Scribe, Stover, and carpenter Rod Suydam shared comments from visitors to the hospital about the power of color.

"My great-grandson was hospitalized for several days as an infant," they quoted one woman as saying of a child with a deadly respiratory virus. "He was too young to speak, but he was mesmerized by the colors. We would be in the hallway and he just stared at the pictures and smiled."

Colors play a crucial role in other parts of the hospital environment. Another visitor had this to say:

"The thing I remember most aesthetically was the colorful lighting sconce in each of the rooms. It faded colors in and out and it was incredibly soothing. The purples and blues were lovely. I loved the nurses who just wore pastel scrubs because it helped me focus on the things they said and their kindness."

Stover said color was used in combination with other elements of the environment — the size, shape, location and so on — and also in consideration of the specific area of the hospital and the reasons children were there.

"We acknowledge that their mood, thoughts and feelings might influence their perception of the colors," Stover said. "Red is a great example. Although it is probably not a good choice in surgery or lab waiting rooms, we know red is a favorite color among children and it's probably OK to have a red train in the vending area where kids are thinking about getting a snack, not getting poked."

Design for comfort and healing reaches beyond the hospital and clinic buildings and walls. Scribe has extended the Children's Mercy "look and feel" to ambulances, helicopters and airplanes.

"The Children's Mercy look is comforting," the artist said. "Children who have been here before recognize it and it can help them feel better, no matter what part of the hospital they're in. There is comfort in that familiarity when there is so much uncertainty."

For some patients, the transport vehicles form their first impression of the hospital. Even before they meet the people who will care for them, they see giant ambulances or hear the chopping of a helicopter. If the paint jobs are fun, and the cartoon characters are cheery and familiar, it can help reduce stress even before the children arrive at the hospital.

Emily Falkenrheh, a nurse who works for the transport team, told a *Kansas City Star* reporter she had seen firsthand how the artwork helped kids.

"We see it all the time" she said in a 2016 article. "We'll bring out a hesitant patient who's afraid and they'll see the ambulance and it brings them peace. Oftentimes, you'll see them physically relax. I've had kids not shut up about it the whole ride to the hospital."

In addition to Scribe and the Child Life specialists, Children's Mercy carpenters, electricians, painters, engineers and others in the maintenance department play an important role in designing and developing the healing environment.

For instance, Suydam, a carpenter with 25 years' experience at Children's Mercy, goes out of his way to help ideas come to life. When a Child Life Specialist in the Dialysis Unit wished for a teaching tool, Suydam used spare and broken-down parts and some plywood to build a scale-model dialysis machine, complete with blinking lights and authentic sounds.

Architects get into the act as well. Prisms that reflect different colored lights onto the walls line a hallway that includes the Art Galaxy, where patients' art is on display. The "star dome" in the rotunda of the main lobby of Children's Mercy Hospital is a favorite spot. There, a panel of buttons allows visitors to change the colors of the sky-like ceiling above them.

"We get great joy to be able to work with Scribe and make a room into a place of wonder and fascination," Suydam said. "Once we finish … we take a step back and watch the reaction of the kids as they walk in the door, walk down the halls or push the buttons that bring an interactive mural to life. When their eyes light up, when they smile, we gain a feeling of fulfillment. At the end of the day we are able to clock out and go home knowing that we contributed to the mental well-being and physical healing of a child."

This is proof positive that patient care — and psychosocial care at that — is everyone's job at Children's Mercy, regardless of the job title.

"I'm a fierce fighter for the idea that everyone is on equal footing," Scribe told *The Kansas City Star*. "It's pretty obvious that someone who does heart surgery on kids is an incredible person, but the people who are doing the janitorial work and working behind the scenes — they make the world go round."

The hospital, of course, is not just a big art museum and is not overflowing with attention-grabbing features. Stover said it was important to build visual resting places for children and their families. They want to avoid overwhelming and overstimulating patients.

The success of their work is part of the reason Scribe, Stover and Suydam made their presentation at the national conference of the Association of Child Life Professionals. Their talk was called "Designed to Heal: A collaborative approach to enhancing pediatric hospital environments." A full house of more than 100 attendees peppered them with questions during and after the presentation.

Even outsiders can see the impact of incorporating art and design into a healing environment like Children's Mercy. *The Kansas City Star* article from 2016 by reporter David Frese included this description:

"Children's Mercy is perhaps one of the best places on earth to spend some of your worst moments. While the hallways are often filled with crying kids, worried moms who hold their babies extra tight and pallid dads staring off into the middle distance, the walls provide relief, distraction or maybe just a smile."

The real proof of the success of their efforts, of course, is in the reaction of the children and their families to the environment so lovingly and purposefully built. One mom summed it up:

"From the moment we pull up at one of the hospitals and the children can see the artwork, they immediately calm down. I cannot express how much this helps me as a parent and I could never thank you enough! I can't even count how many times a tear has dried up due to having the distraction of the artwork."

Donald Ross aka Scribe

Real Life:
Three patients, three families,
one hospital.

The Bickford family. Benjamin, in front, required open heart surgery when he was six weeks old.

REAL LIFE
....

Parents are part of the team

Carey Bickford has found a way to turn adversity into advocacy. Lots of parents and children are better for it.

In early 2012, Bickford and her husband, Austin, had good jobs and a new home in the suburbs, and Carey was pregnant with their first child, a boy. Life was good.

Then Carey went into labor six weeks early. She had an emergency C-section. Her blood pressure spiked, and her baby was whisked away to a neonatal intensive care unit.

"For the first few days, we thought Benjamin was just early," she recalled in 2018. On Day Five, Dr. Stephen Kaine, a cardiologist from Children's Mercy came into her room, saying the Bickfords' son would have to be taken to Children's Mercy.

"He had a complex congenital heart defect and would need open heart surgery," she said. "In the space of days, everything we had envisioned for life with our newborn was turned on its head. There is no school or parenting class to prepare you for that."

What followed was weeks in the Neonatal Intensive Care Unit at Children's Mercy. Benjamin had open heart surgery at six weeks of age to repair *truncus arteriosus*, a rare, congenital heart disease. He would have two more major heart operations and four other surgeries in the weeks, months and years to come.

In those early weeks in the hospital — although she was battling through her own sleep deprivation and emotional rollercoaster — Bickford couldn't help but notice what was going on around her.

"Sometimes, I would begin to (feel sorry for myself)," she said, "and then I'd look and see the 15-year-old single mom with a newborn in the NICU, from a hundred miles away with little family support because grandma can't get off work. I realized just how lucky I was.

"No parent is mentally prepared to handle something like this. How can you be? But as an English-speaking, college-educated woman in my late 20s, in a stable marriage, with a flexible job and financial resources — there weren't numerous other hurdles that we were trying to overcome while trying to focus on the health of our child."

As Benjamin approached his surgery date, Carey and Austin Bickford and Carey's mother took shifts rocking the child nearly around the clock. It seemed to keep him stable and comforted. At the time, Children's Mercy policy did not allow visitors in the NICU overnight; parents were not considered visitors, but Benjamin's grandmother was.

"Some staff members would allow her to be there, and others asked her to leave," Bickford recalls. "We had to push back: Is this really harmful? It seems to help Benjamin. It's helping our peace of mind and she wasn't preventing anyone from doing their work. We needed to find a balance between family well-being and medical necessity."

Spending all those hours in the hospital opened Bickford's eyes to the "practice" of medicine.

"The doctors and nurses are superheroes, but they are also human. Medical staff can't possibly know everything, and that's why parents are an important part of the health care team. They are the experts in their fields, but we are the experts on our kids. We're with them 24/7."

Today, Benjamin is a thriving and energetic 5-year-old getting ready to enter kindergarten. Bickford turned her newfound expertise into helping other parents. She calls it an act of gratitude.

She joined the Family Advisory Board and served as Chair in 2017-2018. She knows firsthand that it's important for families to be included on the team.

"Navigating the world of having a sick child can be extremely complicated: coordinating schedules for clinic visits, making countless phone calls to insurance companies and finding child care that can accommodate their needs," she said. "There are many wonderful staff members dedicated to making it easier — but I think we can do more, and I think parents who have been there are some of the richest resources to help."

The role of parents in care and particularly the role of the Family Advisory Board, has evolved greatly since the 1990s. Initially, only a few parents were invited to be involved and their involvement was limited. Over time, at the insistence of both parents and hospital leadership, parents now have a bona fide role in recommending and evaluating processes, policies and procedures practiced at the hospital.

The Family Advisory Board acts as an oversight group for several other Patient and Family Advisory Councils critical to the hospital's operations. In addition to the three councils for teen patients and one for Spanish-speaking families, other councils serve specific patients and families in cardiology, cystic fibrosis, food allergies, inflammatory bowel disease, the intensive care nursery, tracheostomy and rare diseases.

Bickford knows Children's Mercy is committed to the highest levels of patient- and family-centered psychosocial care. She has seen great improvements in her time at the hospital and she and other parent advocates push for even more.

Grandparents, for instance, are now allowed.

"One area I would like to see additional improvement in is support for the mental health of the parents," Bickford said. "While we weren't in need of 'traditional social work support,' I still suffered from what I now believe to have been post-partum depression/post-traumatic stress disorder, and I really could have used someone reaching out to me six months later to say, 'How are you doing?'

"I realize that children's hospitals are focused on the health of the children — and shouldn't necessarily be in adult care. But healthy parents are a vital part of healthy kids, and there is a need for it to be addressed. I believe working together we can find a way."

The Freeman family. Jackie suffers a rare condition that required many surgeries.

REAL LIFE
....

The hits keep coming

Kim Freeman, mother of one child and pregnant with another, distinctly remembered the feeling as she left the high-risk obstetrics office. The doctors had just confirmed that her unborn baby daughter had a heart defect and a cleft lip.

Freeman was being referred to the Fetal Health Center at Children's Mercy.

"I walked out of that building and into a different world," she said. "You know something's not right. But you have no concept. This is not what you want."

A bit more than two years later, as she retold the story, her emotions were still raw. Tears clouded her eyes at some of the memories. But she also smiled when she described all the things little Jackie Freeman endured.

Freeman knew that the Fetal Health Center, with its intimacy and its wide range of services focused on high-risk babies, was the right place for her and her family.

"It's personalized," she said, "and I felt like the people really get it."

She met the medical staff and knew she was in the right place.

Kim and her husband, John, found instant relief with the social workers.

"We could talk to them. And that is so important because we felt very alone. It's very isolating. I was scared. Nobody understands. Your friends don't understand. They have healthy babies. But the social workers and talking with people who have been there, that makes you feel not so alone."

When Jackie was born in December 2015, it was just the beginning of the family's journey. In addition to the heart defect and cleft lip, doctors also found a cleft palate. Feeding was an issue immediately. So was respiratory distress.

"The hits just kept coming," Freeman said.

On the second or third day of little Jackie's life, the medical team met. Freeman remembered sitting in a conference room surrounded by people in scrubs and white lab coats. There were people from neonatology, cardiology, surgery and genetics. They all talked about Jackie's medical condition, which had a name: CHARGE syndrome.

The name, when it was first used in the early 1980s, represented letters in Coloboma of the eye, Heart defects, Atresia of the choanae, Retardation of Growth and development, and Ear abnormalities and deafness. The syndrome is rare: One in 10,000 cases or so.

The host of possible complications was long, and it was impossible to know which ones would affect Jackie. Freeman was cautioned against looking it up on the Internet because it could overwhelm her. She did, anyway. Jackie would need surgery — lots of surgery. Freeman and her husband, John, listened as long as they could. It was overwhelming. It was too much. When someone asked, "Do you have any questions?" Freeman said she didn't have a clue. She wanted to run away and cry.

"How is this even possible?" she thought to herself.

Freeman said she continued to find comfort in her social worker, who had helped the Freemans in Fetal Health and had come over to help during their NICU stay to provide continuity and familiarity. At the very least, Kim knew she wasn't alone.

After the initial shock, Freeman said, her family went into "survival mode." She said her background in nursing might have helped steel her for what they were facing:

"It's all you can do."

Jackie made it past her second birthday. She survived four surgeries in the first 18 months of her life, to repair her heart and lip and palate and hip. She still suffers seizures. After a particularly frightening one, she visited the world's only CHARGE Syndrome Clinic, in Cincinnati, Ohio. She had 13 appointments in four days.

Jackie is legally blind and uses glasses. She is deaf in her left ear. She struggles with balance and is working hard to learn how to walk independently; she uses a walker. Each child with CHARGE is unique and the effects vary greatly. Jackie has done remarkably well, but it's impossible to know what the future holds.

Freeman is proud of her daughter and her big brother, Weston, whose life also has changed.

"I was so emotional about Weston, too," she said. "What will this take away from him? I thought I was prepared for Jackie, being a nurse, but what about Weston?"

As it turns out he has adjusted pretty well, she said, but as a 4-year-old he doesn't fully grasp that his sister is far different from the way he was.

He also happens to think Children's Mercy is a fun place, with its playrooms, new toys all the time, a Child Life specialist to pay him special attention and even presents for Christmas one year when Jackie was an inpatient.

"He was especially spoiled by Children's Mercy that day," Freeman recalls, "along with Jackie, which truly helped so much since it was no fun being in the hospital on Christmas. But seeing them happy and showered with gifts made it a little bit easier."

Freeman is also happy with the care she received at Children's Mercy, especially the family-centered touches such as the social workers, sibling support and parent-to-parent programs.

That's why she joined the hospital's Family Advisory Board in spring 2018 as part of her plan to "give back." She wants to give back and help serve others.

At home, at night, when the kids are in bed, the new normal envelopes the Freeman household.

"When the dust settles, that's when we struggle," she said. "Reality hits. It changes you. But you keep pushing through. You have to."

Rhonda Meers with Michael, who suffered a brain tumor.

REAL LIFE
....

"In the front lines of a war"

They call him Lucky Sam. It's a nickname he picked up in college and it has stuck with him all these years.

Which is more than a little surprising, considering that Sam Meers had to watch his young son and then his wife die from cancer less than a year apart.

"Just the other day," Meers recounted in 2018, "I passed someone in the stairwell at work and she said, 'You always seem so happy.'

"I look at it this way: none of us gets out of here alive. And it's events like I've been through that make you realize how fortunate you really are."

It wasn't exactly easy to get to that philosophy of peacefulness and serenity. In October 1995, Sam and his wife, Rhonda, learned that their 6-month-old son, Michael, had a brain tumor. The couple and 6-year-old daughter, Katherine, found themselves with a new home away from home: Children's Mercy.

"The news is devastating," Meers recalls. "The doctors have the worst jobs in the world. They have to tell you that your child is sick."

He remembers one meeting with perhaps 30 people: doctors, nurses and other staff people in a room. Michael had already had two brain surgeries. More surgeries and treatments were being discussed. Strategies were weighed. Odds were discussed.

"It's like we were on the front lines of a war and we never got a break. Never."

To make matter worse, just a month after Michael's diagnosis Rhonda Meers was diagnosed with breast cancer. There were times, Sam Meers remembers, when Rhonda and Michael were undergoing chemotherapy on the same day at different hospitals.

"We were fighting a war on multiple fronts," he said.

At home, Meers found himself giving Michael medicine that needed precise measurements. Too little and it wouldn't do its job. Too much and the consequences could have been dire.

"I've never been so terrified," he said. "If I screw this up, he dies. This is why nothing rattles me now."

Less than a year after the diagnosis, in the summer of 1996, Michael began a 97-day stretch of hospitalization. It was exhausting for Michael and for the Meers family. Sam, who owned a small advertising agency at the time, remembered sitting in the hospital room trying to work on an ad campaign: "You move in and do the best you can do."

With life in tatters, Meers said, he tried to provide a little bit of normal life for his daughter. He remembers some of the Children's Mercy staff who helped care for daughter Katherine while she visited.

"The greatest help, the greatest comfort, came from the nurses," he said, rattling off names that he remembered 20 years later. "They provide a sense of continuity. They get to know you and your family."

All this care, of course, came with a cost. After a year, Meers said, Michael's medical bills topped $1 million. Rhonda's employer, Hallmark Cards, told the family not to worry about it. They'd take care of Michael.

"It's bigger than Children's Mercy," Meers said. "It's the whole community that you are surrounded with."

Despite the best efforts of many, Michael's cancer was too much. He died in

April 1997. A short 16 months later, cancer also took his mom.

"Life is too short," Meers said. "I've seen it."

Even with the death of his son, Meers was not done with Children's Mercy. He served as both a paid and volunteer consultant on a variety of communications and marketing efforts, including helping pull together the "Listening, Leading, Learning" cultural transformation report for the Robert Wood Johnson Foundation in 2006. His passion for health care helped transform his business.

Perhaps more telling, though, was that Meers and his family endowed the Michael Meers Scholarship for nurses in the cancer unit where the Meers family was cared for. Each year in May for Nurses' Month, when Children's Mercy awards scholarships, Meers is there to say thank you. Katherine often joins him, as does his wife, Julie. In 2018, Meers spoke at the ceremony about something he knew all too well: resilience.

"I want to get back to the point where I can take some things for granted," he said in his soft-spoken manner. "But nothing can close these chapters. I expect the worst and when it doesn't happen, then I've had a good day."

And he can still consider himself Lucky Sam.

Sam Meers with Michael and daughter Katherine.

Source notes

Innumerable sources were vital to the writing and accuracy of this book. Much information was gleaned from interviews that relied on personal memories of people intimately involved with this story. Books, newspapers, academic journals and websites also were consulted. Throughout the text, you will find some sources named and much information attributed. Details follow in this section and in References.

Chapter 1: Much of this information comes from historical documents, many of them online, with care given to include trustworthy sources, such as universities or medical societies. The book *For All Children Everywhere*, published by Children's Mercy in 2017, provides details of the early days of the hospital and its founders as well as background information about other children's hospitals. Other books, including Luther Emmett Holt's *The Care and Feeding of Children*, John B. Watson's *Psychological Care of Infant and Child* and Florence Nightingale's *Notes on Nursing: What it is and What it is Not*, were consulted and provided interesting context for the thinking of their times about children.

Chapter 2: Watson's book surfaces again in this chapter, as well as newspaper articles and an academic paper written about his philosophy. Web-based sources provided much information about Erik Erickson, including the sites of Harvard University, Wikipedia, SimplyPsychology, the Very Well Mind and the Erikson Institute. *The New York Times* in its obituary provided considerable information about Benjamin Spock, as did Spock's book. *The Times* was also a valuable source of information about T. Berry Brazelton and Penelope Leach. Books by other pioneers in the field of psychosocial care helped fill in the story of the early days, as did several academic journal articles cited in the text and in the References section of this book. The Association of Child Life Professionals, through its Web site and its archive at Utica College, provided details of the founding of the profession. Richard Thompson's book, *PsychoSocial Research on Pediatric Hospitalization: A Review of the Literature*, pointed us toward much valuable research.

Chapter 3: The story of Children's Mercy came together through personal interviews with staff as part of an Oral History project conducted from 2015 to 2017, including stories from Betty Boyd, Ramona Lindsey, Karen Cox and Dane Sommer. Other personal interviews that contributed to this chapter were with Daryl Lynch, Debbie Kerr, Alan Gamis and Heather Brungardt. Many hospital policy documents, scope of service agreements and more, including those related to the Children and Youth Program and the early days of the Social Work Department, were vital to this chapter.

Chapter 4: *For All Children Everywhere* provided the story of the hiring of Randall L. O'Donnell, PhD, in 1993. Personal interviews with Dr. O'Donnell over his tenure at Children's Mercy, as well as a recorded presentation from 2004, contributed the details of his formative experiences. His dissertation was consulted and provided detail on previous studies on the effects of hospitalization on children. His book, *Nurturing Leadership*, offered anecdotes and examples of his management philosophy. Interviews with Karen Cox and Stacey Koenig included details of Dr. O'Donnell's early days at Children's Mercy and the development of Child Life in Kansas City. Ginny Miller graciously told her story of care and of service to Children's Mercy. "Listening, Learning, Leading," the report for the Robert Wood Johnson Foundation, chronicled the Children's Mercy cultural evolution.

Chapter 5: Personal interviews continued to provide the bulk of the content for this chapter, including conversations with Children's Mercy's O'Donnell, Cox, Vicki Clarke, Michael Artman, Denise Dowd, Brad Warady, Jay Portnoy, Daryl Lynch, Emily Goodwin, Kathy Smith, Molly Krager, Child Life Staff, Kaylee Hurt, DeeJo Miller, Cheryl Chadwick, Heather Brungardt, David Cauble, Sarah Soden, Molly Weaver, Julie Aust, Jeff Janda, Angie Richardson and other Human Resources recruiters. Stories created by the Internal Communication team provided content when additional personal interviews were not warranted. A presentation by artist Sandra Ganey on helping medical residents better understand psychosocial care proved helpful.

Chapter 6: Internet research into Adverse Childhood Experiences, particularly through the American Academy of Pediatrics, was most helpful. TED Talk transcripts were used to quote some speakers. Statistics from the National Alliance on Mental Illness helped frame the discussion of mental health. A press release from Children's Mercy on its quality assurance honor was consulted, as was one from the Children's Hospital Association on improving mental health care.

Chapter 7: Almost all of this chapter was based on personal experience of the author observing Children's Mercy staff members in action. Quotes were taken from conversations made during the shadowing process. In some cases, additional interviews (in person or through email) with chaplains, social workers and Child Life specialists filled in stories. The program at the 2018 nurse scholarship awards included some of the stories here. Other stories of nurses providing extraordinary psychosocial care come from a database of DAISY Award winners kept on the

Children's Mercy internal Web site. Cheri Hunt sat for a personal interview. The background of "Listening, Learning, Leading" and personal observations filled in the rest of the stories of this chapter. Internal documents related to volunteers, philanthropy and an interview with one of the Philanthropy department directors, Phil Watson, were also beneficial.

Chapter 8: This chapter, looking into the future, required a bit of soothsaying and the topics included here are based on the best judgment of the authors of this book. Karen Hill and others at the Children's Hospital Association offered time and expertise to point us in the right direction. Karen Sheehan at Lurie Children's Hospital in Chicago graciously offered her time and her stories. Margo Quiriconi, the Children's Mercy director of community health initiatives, offered her perspective during an in-person interview, as did John Lantos, the Children's Mercy bioethicist. Historical data was collected from the Corporation for Public Broadcasting website to provide context to current work. The team at the Center for Community Connections provided a tour and explained its members' expertise on helping families beyond their immediate medical needs. Internal newsletters included stories of a variety of new innovative programs, including transitioning to adult care, and the work at Operation Breakthrough. Interviews with Carey Spain in Social Work at Mark Schmidt of the Blue Valley Schools helped pull together the story of that partnership. An interview with Stacey Koenig and attendance at the Patient Experience national conference in 2018 informed the work in that field. An article by Thomas H. Lee in the *Harvard Business Review* showed how quality in health care can improve financial performance. Spending time with the Home Care staff allowed the authors to write about that experience. Patty Davis, a social worker, provided information and context of the work in Trauma-Informed Care. A presentation by artist Donald "Scribe" Ross, Child Life Specialist Melissa Stover and Carpenter Rod Suydam was used extensively for the "Designed to heal" sidebar.

References

Books

- Nightingale, Florence. *Notes on Nursing: What it is, What it is not.* 1859
- Holt, Luther Emmet. *The Care and Feeding of Children.* 1894
- Watson, John B. *Psychological Care of Infant and Child.* 1928
- Spock, Benjamin. *The Common Sense Book of Baby and Child Care.* 1946
- Eissler, R.S., et al. *The Psychoanalytic Study of the Child.* 1952 (Section of particular note: Freud, Anna. "The Role of Bodily Illness in the Mental Life of Children.")
- Plank, Emma. *Working with Children in Hospitals.* 1962
- Thompson, Richard R. and Stanford, Gene. *Child Life in Hospitals: Theory and Practice.* 1981
- Thompson, Richard H. *PsychoSocial Research on Pediatric Hospitalization and Health Care: A Review of the Literature.* 1985
- Association for the Care of Children's Health. *Psychosocial care of children in hospitals: a clinical practice manual from the ACCH Child Life Research Project.* 1990
- O'Donnell, Randall L. *Nurturing Leadership.* 1992
- Frochich, Mary Ann R., editor. *Music Therapy with Hospitalized Children: A Creative Arts Child Life Approach.* 1996
- Holt Rollins, Judy. *Meeting Children's Psychosocial Needs Across the Health care Continuum.* 2005
- Thompson, Richard H., editor. *The Handbook of Child Life: A Guide for Pediatric Psychosocial Care.* 2009
- McCormally, Thomas. *For All Children Everywhere: Children's Mercy – Kansas City, 1897-2017.* 2017

Journal articles

- Beard, Jessie L. "The Correlation between Nursing and Social Work." American Journal of Nursing. October 1917
- Work, Henry. "Making Hospitalizations Easier for Children." Children. May-June 1956

- Brown, Esther Lucile. "Meeting Parents Psychosocial Needs in the General Hospital." The Annals of the American Academy of Political and Social Science. March 1963
- Briggs, R.F. "Hospitalized Child Faces Emotional Hazards." Hospital Management. May 1967
- Skipper, J.K. and Leonard, R.D. "Stress and Hospitalization: A Field Experiment." Journal of Health and Social Behavior. December 1968
- Hales-Tooke, Ann. "Improving Hospital Care for Children." Children. September-October 1968
- Millar, T.P. "The Hospital and the Pre-School Child." Children. September-October 1970
- Bell, John E. and Bell, Elisabeth A. "Family Participation in Hospital Care for Children." Children. July-August 1970
- Quinton, D. and Rutter, M. "Early Hospital Admissions and Later Disturbances of Behavior: An Attempted Replication of Douglas' Findings." Developmental Medicine and Child Neurology. August 1976
- O'Donnell, Randall L. "Excellence in PsychoSocial Care Can Still Be Achieved in an Era of Cost Containment." Journal of the Association for the Care of Children's Health. Spring 1987
- Burke, Edmund C., "Pediatric History: Abraham Jacobi, MD, the Man and his Legacy." Pediatrics, February 1998
- Felitti, Vincent J., et al. "Relationship of Childhood Abuse and Household Dysfunction to Many of the Leading Causes of Death in Adults: The Adverse Childhood Experiences (ACE) Study." *American Journal of Preventative Medicine.* May 1998
- Johnson, Beverly H. "Family Centered Care: Four Decades of Progress." The Journal of Collaborative Family Health Care. Summer 2000
- Haidet P, Dains JE, Paterniti DA, Hechtel L, Chang T, Tseng E, et al. "Medical student attitudes toward the doctor-patient relationship. Medical Education. June 2002
- Epstein, Ronald L. and Street, Richard L. Jr. "The Values and Value of Patient Centered Care." Annals of Family Medicine. March 2011
- O'Donnell, Randall L.; Cox, Karen, et al. "Redesigning the Health Care System of the Future." Missouri Medicine Magazine. January-February 2006
- Kahn, Joseph J., et al. "A Program to Decrease the Need for Pediatric Sedation for CT and MRI." Applied Radiology. April 2007
- Sparks, L.A, et al. "Parental Holding and Positioning to Decrease Distress in Young Children: A Randomized Controlled Trial." Journal of Pediatric

Nursing. December 2007

- Kaba, R. and Sooriakumaran, P. "The Evolution of the Doctor-Patient Relationship. The International Journal of Surgery. February 2007
- Lacey, C.M., et al. "The Impact of Positioning on Fear during Immunization: Supine versus Sitting up." Journal of Pediatric Nursing. June 2008
- Shonkoff, Jack P., Garner, Andrew, et al. "The Lifelong Effects of Early Childhood Adversity and Toxic Stress." American Academy of Pediatrics. January 2012
- Committee on Psychosocial Aspects of Child and Family Health, et al. "Early Childhood Adversity, Toxic Stress and the Role of the Pediatrician: Translating Developmental Science into Lifelong Health." American Academy of Pediatrics. January 2012
- Mann, Keith J., Hoffman, Amber, Miller, DeeJo, Chadwick Sheryl, Bratcher, Denise. "The Effect of a Patient and Family-Centered Care Curriculum on Pediatrics Residents' Patient Centeredness." Journal of Graduate Medical Education. March 2013
- Scott, Kate M., et al. "Association of Mental Disorders with Subsequent Chronic Physical Conditions: World Mental Health Surveys from 17 Countries." American Medical Association. December 2015
- Wolf, Jason. "The Patchwork Perspective: A New View of Patient Experience." Patient Experience Journal. Vol. 4, Issue 3: 2017
- Christensen, Tiffany. "Rebalancing the Patient Experience: 20 Years of a Pendulum Swing." Patient Experience Journal. Vol. 4, Issue 3: 2017
- O'Connell, Karen and Fritzeen, Jennifer, et al. "Family Presence During Trauma Resuscitation: Family Members' Attitudes, Behaviors and Experiences." American Journal of Critical Care. May 2017
- Dowd, M. Denise; Lantos, John M.; Leifer, Loring; O'Malley, Donna; Woods-Jaeger, Briana A.; Cox, Karen; Westbrook David H., et al. "Addressing Toxic Stress from Adverse Childhood Experiences through a Collaboration between a Children's Hospital and a Community Organization." Current Problems in Pediatric and Adolescent Health Care. Sept. 2017
- Wolf, Jason. "What Patient Experience Can Learn from Child Life Professionals." The Beryl Institute. 2018
- Biblow, Rachel and Toomey, Sara. "Partners for Excellence: Committed to Meaningful Partnerships with Patients and Families in Pediatrics." Patient Experience Journal. Vol. 5, Issue 2: 2018
- Taff, Kathryn, Chadwick, Sheryl and Miller, DeeJo. "Family Experience Tracers: Patient Family Advisory Led Interviews Generating Detailed

Qualitative Feedback to Influence Performance Improvement. Patient Experience Journal. Vol. 5, Issue 2: 2018

Presentations/talks

The following are all attributed to O'Donnell, Randall L.
- "Children's Needs and Health Care Reform." Testimony on behalf of the National Association of Children's Hospitals and Related Institutions before the Subcommittee on Health for Families and the Uninsured Committee on Finance, U.S. Senate. Washington, D.C. November 1993
- "Excellence in Psychosocial Care in an Era of Cost Containment: Challenges and Realities," Brazelton Lecture, Association for the Care of Children's Health 30th Annual Conference. Boston. May 1995
- "When It's Your Child," Whiteman Air Force Base. February, 1999; Carthage, Missouri, United Way. September 2000; Kansas City Mercury Club. May 2002
- "A CEO's Perspective on the Importance of Psychosocial Care." 9th Annual Midwest Child Life Networking Conference. November 2003; Grand Rounds at Children's Hospital of Wisconsin. September 2004
- "Leadership at Children's Mercy Hospitals & Clinics: The Priority of Psychosocial Care."Annual Conference of CEOs from children's hospitals in China. Harbin, China. January 2009
- "Children's Mercy Hospitals and Clinics Cultural Cornerstones." National Children's Hospital's Presidents Conference. Guangzhou, China. September 2009
- "A Vision for Pediatric Genomic Medicine at Children's Mercy Hospitals and Clinics." Southern Medical University. Guangzhou, China. May 2011
- "Nursing Excellence: Promoting Psychosocial Care anjd The Magnet Program." Guangzhou Women and Children's Medical Center Nursing Conference. Guangzhou, China. May 2011

Other presentations referenced:
- Prugh, D.G., Staub, E., Sands, H.H, Kirschbaum, R.M. and Lenihan, E.A. "A Study of the Emotional Reactions of Children and Families to Hospitalization and Illness." American Journal of Orthopsychiatry. 1952
- Balint, Enid. "The Possibility of Patient Centered Medicine." American Psychiatric Association. March 1968
- Burke Harris, Nadine. "How Childhood Trauma affects health across a lifetime." TEDMED. 2014

- Dowd, M. Denise. "Leadership is an Activity, Not a Position: Your Legacy, Your Future." Society for Social Work Leadership in Healthcare. October 2015
- Brungardt, Heather. "Innovation on Social Work Leadership." Society for Social Work Leadership in Healthcare. October 2016
- Ross, Donald, Stover, Missy and Suydam, Ron. "Designed to Heal: A collaborative Approach to Enhancing Pediatric Hospital Environments." Association of Child Life Professionals. May 2018
- Ganey, Sandra and McIntire, Caroline. "A Psychosocially Inclusive Resident Education Model." Association of Child Life Professionals. May 2018
- Caruso Brown, Amy. "Is Being Treated at a Children's Hospital a Right or a Privilege?" Children's Mercy – Kansas City Bioethics Center. May 2018

Other sources

- O'Donnell, Randall L. "The Psychological Effects of Childhood Hospitalization: Implications for Pediatric Health Care Delivery." Thesis submitted in partial fulfillment of requirements for PhD in Hospital and Health Administration, the University of Iowa. July 1977
- Lawson, Carol. "Growing up with Help from Penelope Leach." *The New York Times*. 1991
- Bradelton, T. Berry. Oral history. American Academy of Pediatrics. Feb. 19, 1997
- Pace, Eric. "Benjamin Spock, World's Pediatrician, Dies at 94." Obituary. *The New York Times*. March 17, 1998
- Talbot, Margaret. "The Lives They Lived: Benjamin Spoke, MD; A Spock-Marked Generation." *The New York Times Magazine,* Jan. 3, 1999
- Houk, Suzanne. "Psychological Care of Infant and Child: A Reflection of its Author and his Times." Paper in Developmental Psychology. Duquesne University. March 2000
- "The First Measured Century." BJW Inc., in association with New River Media. 2000
- Acocella, Joan. "Mother's Helpers: A Century of Child-Rearing Manuals." *The New Yorker*. May 5, 2003
- Planetree Inc., the Picker Institute. "Patient Centered Care Improvement Guide." October 2008
- Mesure, Susie. "Babies Change Your Life," *The Independent*. May 5, 2010
- "Spock at 65: Five Ideas that Changed America." *Parenting*. July 14, 2011

- American Academy of Pediatrics, "Pediatrics 101: A Resource Guide." 2011
- Ryan, Britta. "A Qualitative Study of Medical Social Workers' and Nurses' Perceptions on Effective Interprofessional Collaboration." Master of Social Work Clinical Research Paper. St. Catherine University. May 2012
- McLeod, S.A. "Erik Erikson." SimplyPsychology.org. 2013
- American Academy of Pediatrics Committee on Hospital Care and Association of Child Life Professionals. "Policy Statement on Child Life Services." May 2014
- Reisman, Anna. "Hospitals need a checklist for the patient experience." KevinMD.com blog. January 2016
- Lee, Thomas H. "How US Health Care Got Safer by Focusing on the Patient Experience." *Harvard Business Review*. May 31, 2017
- "The Top Six Myths about the Social Determinants of Health." Lexis/Nexis Health. August 2017
- Blue Cross Blue Shield Institute Annual Benefit Report. 2017
- Wolf, Jason A. "What Patient Experience can learn from Child Life Professionals." The Beryl Institute. 2018
- "Screening for Social Determinants of Health: Children's Hospitals Respond." Children's Hospital Association. 2018
- "Erikson's Stages of Psycho-Social Development." Wikipedia. Downloaded Jan. 30, 2018.
- Blakeslee, Sandra. "Dr. T. Berry Brazelton, who Explored Babies' Mental Growth, Dies at 99." Obituary. *The New York Times*. March 14, 2018
- Klass, Perri. "How Dr. T. Berry Brazelton Shaped Pediatrics." *The New York Times*. March 15, 2018
- Erikson Institute. "Erik Erikson biography." Downloaded March 16, 2018
- Erikson Institute Strategic Plan, 2016-2018. Downloaded March 16, 2018
- T. Berry Brazelton biography. Wikipedia. Downloaded March 20, 2018
- Penelope Leach biography. Wikipedia. Downloaded March 21, 2018
- "World Mental Health Day 2018." World Health Organization Website. October 10, 2018.

Children's Mercy documents/reports

- "Listening, Leading, Learning: The Cultural Evolution of Children's Mercy Hospitals and Clinics 1995-2006." Prepared at the request of the Robert Wood Johnson Foundation, 2006
- Community Needs Health Needs Assessment Implementation Strategy. 2016-2019

- "All About Me: A guide to taking charge of your health care." 2016
- Social Work Annual Reports. 2016, 2017
- Community Benefit Report 2017
- Annual Reports 2017:
  - Family Advisory Boards
  - Patient Advocate department
  - Language Services department
  - Care Continuum department
  - Council on Violence Prevention
  - Equity and Diversity department
  - Community Programs: Home-based Family Support Programs
- Psychosocial Services Division Overview. 2017
- Psychosocial Services Stewardship report. 2018

About the Authors

Thomas McCormally, MS, was an award-winning journalist at Kansas City area newspapers 1979-1993. He has since worked at children's hospitals, first in communications and public relations and currently as historian at Children's Mercy Kansas City. He first learned about psychosocial care as a college-age volunteer in his mom's Head Start classroom. His first book, *For All Children Everywhere*, is a history of Children's Mercy and was published in 2017.

Randall L. O'Donnell, PhD, has devoted his professional life to studying and promoting psychosocial care at children's hospitals. He served in leadership roles at The Children's Hospital of Buffalo (1977-1980); Arkansas Children's Hospital (1980-1993); and Children's Mercy Kansas City (1993-2018), where he was the longest serving President and Chief Executive Officer in the hospital's 122-year history. His book "Nurturing Leadership" was published in 1992. He earned numerous professional awards and has spoken worldwide on the topics of leadership and psychosocial care.

Index